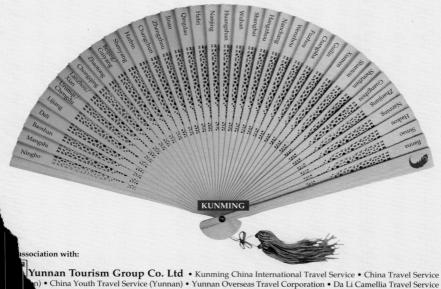

YUNNAN

By Patrick R. Booz

Distribution in the United Kingdom, Ireland and Europe by
Hi Marketing Ltd, 38 Carver Road, London SE24 9LT, UK
ISBN: 962-217-210-5
British Library Cataloguing-in-Publication Data
A catalogue record for this book is available from the British Library

This edition first published in North America in 1997
by Passport Books, 4255 W. Touhy Avenue
Lincolnwood (Chicago), Illinois 60646-1975, USA
T 847 679 5500   F 847 679 2494
ISBN: 0-8442-9664-3
Library of Congress Catalogue Card Number: on file

PASSPORT BOOKS

a division of *NTC/Contemporary Publishing Company*
Lincolnwood, Illinois USA

Grateful acknowledgement is made to the following authors and publishers for permissions granted:
In Lijiang © 1987 Bruce Chatwin
Editors: Stefan Cucos, Kevin Bishop
Designer: Harvey Symons
Maps: Tom Le Bas
Cover concept: Aubrey Tse

Front cover: Wong How-Man
Photography: Magnus Bartlett 5, 8, 12, 29, 40–1, 53, 66–7, 78–9, 86–7, 91, 94–5, 97, 117,
124–5, 133, 141, 145, 172 (top left), 173 (top right, bottom), 181, 187; China Guides Series
56–7, 113, 153; Jing Zhang 70; Mao Baige 48, 108–9, 128–9; Wong How-Man 13, 40–1, 132,
140, 149, 157, 168–9, 172 (top right, bottom), 173 (top left), Tom Nebbia 177
Chinese woodcuts appear courtesy of China Books and Periodicals Inc.

Production by Twin Age Limited, Hong Kong
Printed in Hong Kong

Nuosi Yi minority woman from the Lijiang district

Contents

Special Topics

Maps

Literary Excerpts

Map Key

(Red) ———	Main road	⅄ Mosque
– – – –	Railway	∏ City gate
—— – ——	National boundary	*(Red)* ✚ Hospital
—— - ——	Provincial boundary	† Church
....	Footpath	■ Hotel
		★ Restaurant

Introduction

Yunnan is the sixth largest of China's 28 provinces, similar in size to California or Sweden. It contains more variety than either of them, with towering, ice mountains adjoining Tibet and Burma in the northwest and lush jungles bordering Laos and Vietnam in the south. Half of all China's animal and plant species can be found somewhere in Yunnan, and its nearly 40 million people include members of 25 different ethnic groups—a third of its total population.

Geologically, Yunnan is an offshoot of Tibet, whose soaring tableland spreads eastwards, creating a plateau of red earth over a mile high (about 2,000 metres). Yunnan's southern latitude, astride the Tropic of Cancer, combined with its high altitude, gives it a gentle climate. Winters are mild and sunny; summers bring cool monsoon rains.

In western Yunnan mighty ranges fan south from Tibet's border, channelling some of Asia's greatest rivers through immensely deep canyons. The Salween, the Mekong and the Yangzi race side by side far below the snowcapped peaks, barely 80 kilometres (50 miles) apart. Movements in the earth's unstable crust continue to thrust the mountains upwards and subject Yunnan to periodic earthquakes.

Fertile lake basins lie in geological faults on the plateau, where movement has caused the earth's crust to pull apart and form extensive down-dropped areas. These form the agricultural, political and cultural heart of the province. Kunming's Lake Dianchi and the surrounding plain is the largest such area. The red soil produces rice in abundance, along with year-round vegetable crops, and teas that are considered to be among the best in China.

Botanical gardens in Kunming and in tropical Xishuangbanna display an amazing array of plant life. Many valuable herbs, staples of Chinese medicine, originate in the mountains. Botanists come to see the camellias and rhododendrons, the province's special pride, since all species of these splendid shrubs trace their ancestry to Yunnan. Wild animals and birds also exist in great variety, though population pressure and destruction of habitat threaten them. Elephants, though rare, still roam the jungles near Laos and Burma. Bears and snow leopards are sometimes seen in the eastern Himalayas. Sadly, many rare animals are being hunted to extinction for their fur or for those parts that are valued in medicine.

Yunnan has a very long history. Mankind first appeared at least a million—or perhaps as much as three million—years ago. For many years Peking Man, discovered in 1921, was the oldest known example of prehistoric man in China—until geologists began planning the Kunming-Chengdu railway in 1965 and saw Yunnan's fossils. An old cowherd from the village of Yuanmou, northwest of

Kunming, mentioned that villagers had been grinding up 'dragon bones' as medicine for years. The surveyors, recognizing the common name for fossils, found a deep gully near Yuanmou whose cliff-like walls contained quantities of ancient mammal fossils. Among them, a young geologist discovered two human front teeth. The Forest of Earthen Hills (Zhima Lin) in Banguo, outside Yuanmou, is now famous for its abundance of animal and plant fossils.

Palaeontologists from China's Academy of Sciences named this ancient man *Homo erectus yuanmouensis,* or Yuanmou Man. The formation of the teeth convinced them that he was Peking Man's ancestor, China's oldest known humanoid. Later excavations in 1973 indicated that Yuanmou Man knew the use of fire, and shared a lakeside plain with primitive forms of elephant and an early ancestor of the horse, extinct species that helped to date him.

In 1988 further palaeontological evidence came to light when scientists from the Yunnan Provincial Museum unearthed the fossil skull of *Ramapithecus hudiensis* at Hudieliangzi, also near Yuanmou. This great discovery filled in the human fossil record of the Pliocene epoch and provided evidence that a complete process of evolution from early hominid to man has taken place in China. This find advanced significantly the story begun by the discovery on Yuanmou Man.

Vast expanses of time passed with no record to show how Yunnan became populated or how its people lived. For the first thousand years of China's recorded history, it was known only as a savage region inhabited by non-Chinese tribes, beyond the reach of Chinese civilization. In 1955 a sophisticated Bronze-Age culture was discovered when 48 untouched tombs, dating from 1200 BC, were found at the southern end of Lake Dianchi (see page 58–63). These ancient people, living in a kingdom named Dian, described their daily life in great detail, using bronze figurines to depict miniature scenes on the lids of their huge treasury vessels. The people of Dian were slave-owners and head-hunters; they took part in an animal cult featuring bulls, reminiscent of their close contemporaries in King Minos's Crete; the Dian folk also practised advanced methods of agriculture and were fine artists as well.

The first recorded Chinese invasion was in 339 BC, when a prince of the Yangzi River valley sent his general over the mountains to conquer the 'southwest barbarians'. The campaign lasted ten years, during which his return route to China was cut by the prince's rivals. When the general found himself isolated, he set himself up as the King of Dian in a capital near present-day Kunming. For two centuries his descendants ruled the kingdom, completely cut off from China, and intermarried with the Dian people.

The great Han Dynasty ruled China from 206 BC to AD 220 and struck up an important silk trade with Europe. Citizens of the Roman Empire quickly developed a taste for silk togas. One branch of the transcontinental trade, known as the

Southwest Silk Road, ran through Yunnan to India. The Han emperor, wishing to control the entire trade route, launched the second Chinese invasion of Yunnan. The King of Dian welcomed the invaders, hoping his new allies would help him to subdue neighbouring tribes. He thereupon received an imperial seal recognizing Dian as a tributary state. But the Chinese army could not get past Yunnan's formidable western mountains and eventually withdrew. Dian's tribal chiefs ruled in the name of the emperor and when the Han Dynasty finally collapsed, Yunnan continued on its own course as before. In time, the Dian kingdom weakened and tribes from the south seized power. In the eighth century, six princes ruled the southwest. One of them is said to have travelled north to China, which was enjoying a golden age under the Tang Dynasty (618–907). When asked where he came from, the prince replied that his home was south of Sichuan's rainy weather - at which the emperor dubbed the land Yunnan, meaning 'South of the Clouds'. (This tale is disputed by some historians, who claim that the Han emperor chose the name many centuries earlier.)

In 732, the most ambitious prince treacherously invited the other five to a banquet. When they were suitably drunk, he set fire to the wooden banquet hall, killing them all. The triumphant prince seized their lands and named himself Nanzhao, Prince of the South. For five centuries, the Nanzhao Kingdom and its successor, the Kingdom of Dali, remained strong and independent, on a par with China and Tibet, its warring neighbours. Its capital was Dali, on Erhai Lake in western Yunnan.

The kingdom came to an end in 1253 at the hands of Kublai Khan, the famous Mongol, grandson of Genghis Khan. Kublai's efforts in the southwest were part of a great strategy by the Mongols to subdue the Song Dynasty, first taking Yunnan, then pressing the attack from both the north and west. When the Dali Kingdom fell to the Mongol invaders, most of the population fled west and south, leaving an empty land. Kublai Khan's successes were in part due to the help of tough Muslim mercenaries from Persia and Central Asia; he sent these fierce troops to Yunnan, partly to keep them out of mischief, far from the northern capital, but also to repopulate the southwest. The Muslim settlers also served as the emperor's watchdogs against any movements for independence.

Yunnan became a land of foreigners, Muslim and Mongol. It was the last area of China to hold out when the indigenous Ming Dynasty overthrew the Mongols in 1368, thus inviting another invasion. The Ming forces drove out or killed all foreign groups brought in by the cosmopolitan Mongols. Only some of the Muslims were allowed to stay. One such Muslim from Yunnan, Zheng He, rose to become the new emperor's admiral, and a great explorer of the world (see page 182). Ming viceroys in Yunnan built an extensive canal system, added a massive city wall to Yunnanfu (Kunming) and constructed Chinese-style temples.

For centuries, the Ming Dynasty, and the Qing (Manchu) Dynasty that followed it, ruled Yunnan as a colony rather than as a true province of China. It served China as a kind of Siberia, a place of exile for criminals, dissidents, and officials who fell out of favour with the emperor. The actual number of progressive thinkers and intellectuals banished there was relatively small but they brought with them the language, architecture and customs of north China. One lasting sign of their influence is the style of roofs in many central Yunnanese towns, reminiscent of the imperial splendour in Beijing.

A decorative button being sewn onto a tribal garment

In the 18th century, the Qing emperor used Yunnan as a springboard for launching successful military expeditions against the Burmese. Thereafter, ' tribute elephants' carrying jade from Upper Burma and rubies from Mandalay plodded along the old Burma Road to Yunnanfu. There the tribute was transferred to pack horses and sent north to Beijing. Yunnan was still treated as a semi-barbaric colony, only fit for exiles, but along its borders big changes were taking place. Burma soon fell under the influence of the ever-growing British Empire, and the French established themselves in Tonkin, their first step into Indochina. Both European empires eyed Yunnan's rich tin and copper mines covetously.

In 1855, a dispute between Muslim and Chinese miners escalated into a full-scale Muslim rebellion against Chinese rule. It raged on for almost 20 years. Muslims ransacked Kunming's old temples, burned its monasteries, destroyed Buddhist monuments (except for two pagodas), and levelled most public buildings and large private homes. They set up their own capital in Dali. The European powers were quick to take advantage of the chaos in Yunnan. Britain supplied arms to the Muslims through Burma, while France sent arms to the emperor.

Chinese troops finally crushed the rebellion with great cruelty in 1873, slaughtering Muslim men, women and children in Dali and sweeping on to massacre thousands more in smaller towns. Plague broke out, killing many of the survivors. Yunnan was nearly depopulated for the second time in its turbulent history. France and Britain both wangled concessions from the failing Qing Dynasty—the French to build a railway into Yunnan from their new colonial capital in Hanoi, and the British to open trade. In 1911 China became a republic and Yunnan fell into the hands of local warlords.

Japan's invasion of China in 1937 heralded World War II and inflicted immense damage. The upheaval there included the evacuation of factories, universities and government agencies when the Japanese occupied China's east coast. Industries were set up and money poured in. The Burma Road and flights from India funnelled supplies into Yunnan, destined for Allied war bases all over West China. Strategically placed Kunming became a major American base, host to General Chenault's Flying Tigers and General Stilwell's land troops.

The war convinced Yunnan's population that its best interests lay with China. In 1949, there was very little resistance to Chairman Mao's liberation forces. Since then, Yunnan has enjoyed more prosperity than at any time in its history, though remote mountain areas remain among the poorest in all China. Its mines and natural resources have been developed, and modern transportation has overcome its old curse of remoteness and inaccessibility. In the 1990s Yunnan is changing fast, developing links with Southeast Asia and becoming a major entrepôt and tourist destination of Southwest China.

Its natural beauty, healthy climate, and the friendliness of its people have combined to make it one of China's most attractive areas, and a trip through Yunnan is unlike any other in China for the geographic and cultural variety.

Sugar cane in market of Xishuangbanna

Facts For The Traveller

Getting to Yunnan

In the early part of the 20th century, Yunnan was almost inaccessible to foreigners. The arduous, overland trip up the Yangzi River to Chongqing (Chungking) and south through brigand-infested mountains to Kunming was considered too dangerous. Most travellers chose to take the sea route from Hong Kong to Haiphong, in Vietnam, and the French-run railway from Hanoi to Kunming.

Yunnan is tucked into China's southwest corner. It is bounded on the south by Vietnam and Laos, and on the west by Burma. Although it is now reached easily by air or train, a trip there still carries the cachet of remoteness and true adventure.

BY AIR

China Yunnan Airlines offers a comfortable and convenient service direct from Singapore to Kunming, the capital of Yunnan Province. Their modern fleet of Boeing 737s and new wide-body 767s fly from Kunming to 41 regional destinations, including daily flights between Bangkok and Kunming, and thus offer an ideal 'gateway' to China from Southeast Asia.

Flights between Hong Kong and Kunming leave almost daily by either China Southwest Airways or Dragon Air. Kuala Lumpur and Macau will be linked directly with Yunnan in the near future. A long standing weekly flight continues to be maintained between Rangoon and Kunming.

For tourists already inside the country, China Yunnan Airlines run regular flights between Kunming and most major cities in China including Beijing, Guangzhou, Xian, Shanghai, Chengdu and Hangzhou.

BY TRAIN

The engineering feat of linking Yunnan by rail to the rest of China was tremendous, only accomplished in the 1960s and early 1970s. Mountains, ravines and landslides were overcome. Now that trains are safe and comfortable, the railway is a spectacular way to enter Yunnan.

Three classes of accommodation exist on all long-distance trains, known as 'soft sleeper' (first class), 'hard sleeper' (second class) and 'hard seat' (third class). Groups travelling under the care of CITS (China International Travel Service) ride first class; this provides clean, comfortable European-style compartments with four soft berths, a potted plant, lace curtains and porcelain teacups, which all add a quaint charm. Bedding is provided and each carriage has a washing room with running water and a western-style toilet.

Second class, favoured by most budget travellers, provides six berths, three on each side, in a bay opening on the corridor. The middle of the three berths is the best; the bottom berth is used as a seat by all occupants during the day. Bedding is provided and there are overcrowded washing facilities with an Asian-style squat toilet. Second-class travel offers the chance to be a part of Chinese life, where food, companionship and conversation are freely shared, without much discomfort.

Third class is cheap, crowded and uncomfortable. Benches facing each other across a small table are built to seat three adults but frequently hold whole families and their possessions, which overflow into the aisle. Washing facilities and toilets are unmentionable. Most Chinese travel third class.

General Information

VISAS

Everyone must get a visa to go to China, but this is usually an easy, trouble-free process. Tourist visas for individual travellers can be obtained directly through Chinese embassies and consulates, although some embassies are less enthusiastic about issuing them than others. Many travel agents and tour operators around the world can arrange individual visas for their clients. The procedure is simplest in Hong Kong, where innumerable travel agents handle visa applications. Two passport photographs and a completed application form are necessary. Visa fees vary considerably, depending on the source of the visa, and on the time taken to get it. A visa to China can be obtained within a few hours (for a special fee), though more commonly it takes 48 hours.

The visa gives you access to all China's open cities and areas. Internal travel permits (*luxingzhen*) to closed or restricted areas are generally obtained through the Foreign Affairs Bureau or the Public Security Bureau (PSB) in the provincial capital.

Regular business visitors are eligible for a multiple re-entry visa which may be obtained with the help of a business contact in China. Some Hong Kong travel agents can also arrange six-month re-entry visas for regular travellers. Single-entry tourist visas are for one month or three months and can be extended once you are in China.

CLIMATE AND CLOTHING

Yunnan has the best climate in China and Kunming is known throughout the country as 'Spring City' (*chuncheng*). Temperatures there rarely reach freezing in winter, and the days are crisp and sunny. The rainy season lasts from late May through

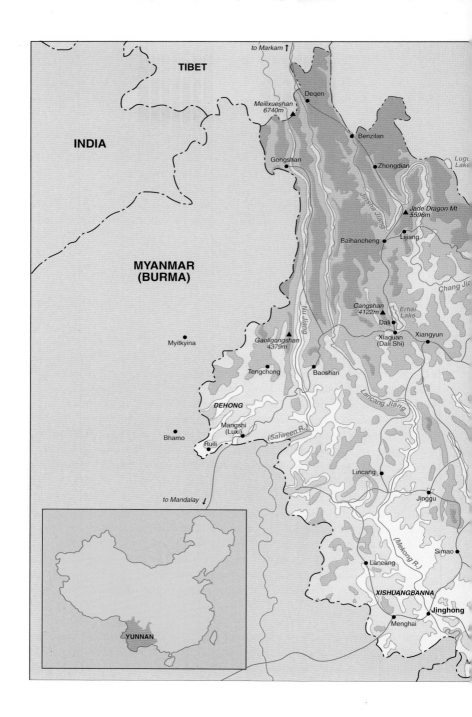

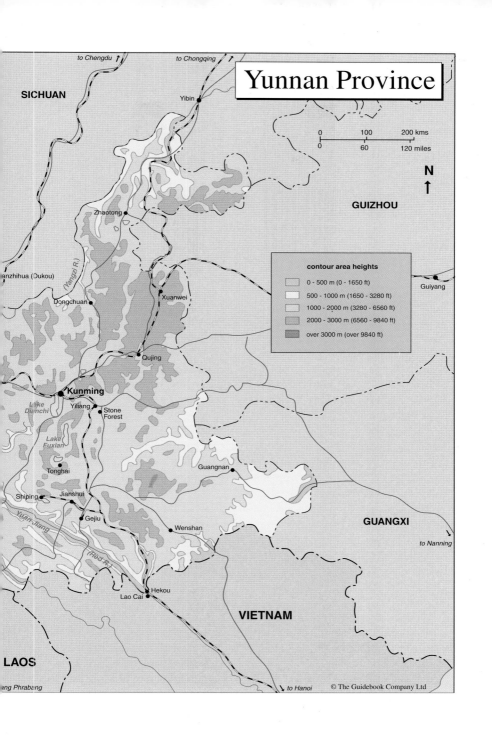

Yunnan Province

SICHUAN

to Chengdu

to Chongqing

Yibin

GUIZHOU

0   100   200 kms
0   60   120 miles

N

Zhaotong

(Yangzi R.)

anzhihua (Dukou)

Guiyang

Dongchuan

Xuanwei

contour area heights

	0 - 500 m (0 - 1650 ft)
	500 - 1000 m (1650 - 3280 ft)
	1000 - 2000 m (3280 - 6560 ft)
	2000 - 3000 m (6560 - 9840 ft)
	over 3000 m (over 9840 ft)

Qujing

Kunming

Lake Dianchi

Yiliang

Stone Forest

Lake Fuxian

Tonghai

Guangnan

Shiping

Jianshui

Yuan Jiang

Gejiu

Wenshan

GUANGXI

(Red R.)

to Nanning

Hekou

Lao Cai

VIETNAM

LAOS

ang Phrabang

to Hanoi

© The Guidebook Company Ltd

August but on most days there is sunshine between the showers. Spring and autumn are sublime. The high altitude causes some fluctuations of temperature, and nights are generally chilly.

Clothing should be simple and consist of layers which can be added or removed as temperatures vary during the day. A sweater and light jacket will be useful and stout, comfortable shoes are recommended. Special items to bring to Yunnan include sunscreen lotion and sun glasses against the intense sunlight, and a hat. The high, dry plateau is likely to cause chapped lips and cracked skin; lip salve and skin cream should not be forgotten.

Travel to the southern part of Yunnan Province requires light, cotton clothing suitable for the tropics. Travellers to Dali, Lijiang or Zhongdian in the northwest of the province should take gloves and a warm coat or jacket between October and March.

TRANSPORTATION

Yunnan's provincial rail system is limited due to the mountainous terrain. Buses are by far the commonest form of transport within Yunnan Province. Although most buses are old and rickety, the system is remarkably extensive and reliable. Kunming is the hub of the system. The main bus station for all long-distance travel within the province is the Passenger Transport Bus Station (Qiche Keyun Zhan) near the Railway Station, at the southern end of Beijing Lu. Other departure points are West Station (Xi Zhan) and East Station (Dong Zhan), and Xiao Xi Men Station (see Kunming map on page 32).

For travellers in groups, China International Travel Service (CITS), Overseas Travel Corporation (OTC) or other travel agencies automatically provide a vehicle as part of the package arrangement. Around Kunming and other cities, taxi fares must be negotiated and agreed upon before beginning the journey. This is important because many tourists are easily cheated.

Hiring vehicles for long-distance travel is possible. This can be done through the major hotels or travel agencies. If you speak Chinese you can discover other means to find transportation. Always settle on the price before beginning your trip, or at least know what the fare per kilometer will be and have this agreed upon in writing. Expect to pay between Rmb 2 and 5 per kilometer, depending on the vehicle.

MONEY

The Chinese currency, referred to as Renminbi or Rmb, meaning 'people's currency', is denominated in *yuan* which are each divided into 10 *jiao*, colloquially called *mao* which are, in turn, each divided into 10 *fen*. There are notes for 100, 50,10, 5, 2 and 1 yuan, small notes for 5, 2 and 1 jiao, and even smaller notes for 5, 2 and 1 fen.

Foreign Exchange Certificates (FECs) were introduced into China in May 1980 as a means of controlling foreign currncy and were issued to all foreigners; **they have now been phased out entirely**. Renminbi are now used throughout China. The exchange rate is approximately US$1=Rmb 8.5.

HOLIDAYS

In contrast to the long calendar of traditional Chinese festivals, modern China now has only three official holidays: May Day,1 October, marking the founding of the People's Republic of China, and Chinese New Year, often called the Spring Festival (*chunjie*), which comes at the lunar new year, usually in late January or early February.

COMMUNICATIONS

Mail in Kunming, incoming and outgoing, is reliable and quite fast if sent by airmail. Telegrams can be sent from post offices, the international telephone service is getting steadily better and is best from large hotels. Faxes are now common.

CUSTOMS

Art objects and antiques obtained in China are often closely scrutinized. Antiques should carry a seal showing that they were bought in an official shop. Contemporary art objects should be accompanied by a receipt. Souvenirs bought on the street are usually allowed to pass, but customs officials have been known to confiscate jewellery or curios if they consider that a tourist has purchased 'too much'. There is a huge amount of smuggling of antiques out of China.

LANGUAGE

Mandarin (*putonghua*, 'common speach') is China's official language, spoken by more than 700 million people. It is the most widely spoken language in the world. Although technically within the Mandarin-speaking region, Yunnan has its own colourful dialect which outsiders find difficult to understand. Most people understand standard Mandarin, and investing in a simple phrasebook will make your trip more enjoyble. See page 182–3.

Food and Drink

Yunnan cuisine, though not yet well known in the West, is one of the best regional eating experiences in China. Many dishes borrow hot, spicy flavours from neighbouring Sichuan. Others, influenced by periodic migrations from provinces such as Jiangsu, Zhejiang and Guangdong, reflect the subtle, rounded taste of eastern and southeastern Chinese cuisine. The year-round availability and variety of vegetables provides a seemingly limitless menu.

Specialities found nowhere else include Xuanwei *huotui*, a strong, tasty, country-cured ham. Unlike in the rest of China, the Yunnanese appreciate certain dairy products. An excellent mild white cheese (*rubing*) is always eaten fried or steamed in combination with ham or vegetables, especially the tender, emerald-green horse-beans (*candou*). In spring and summer eels, caught in the wet rice fields, are a great delicacy and are considered to be among the most nutritious of foods. In Yunnan, eel is usually cooked in a rich brown sauce with garlic and fresh mint. Many varieties of freshwater fish are available, the champion being the Big-headed fish (*datouyu*). Pork is the most widely eaten meat, but because of the province's large Muslim population, beef and mutton are readily found. True carnivores interested in a rare experience might want to try the Sheep and Goat Banquet, which includes some 40 ovine dishes.

Mushrooms appear in great profusion when the rains let up in August. The most highly prized of the dozens of varieties are 'chicken-taste mushroom' (*jizong*) and morel, called 'sheep-stomach mushroom' (*yangduzi*). For vegetable lovers, Yunnan is a joy. Lotus root, bamboo shoots, tender young pea-sprouts, Chinese broccoli, beans of many types, green garlic shoots, just to mention a few, feature in delectable dishes.

Uniquely Yunnanese is the ceramic steam pot, a squat, round, lidded vessel with an internal spout, or chimney, that allows steam to enter and circulate but not escape. Chicken cooked by this technique produces a superior soup entirely from steam and natural juices. This dish, called Steam Pot Chicken (*qiguoji*) comes first on the list of Yunnan's specialities. A remarkable feature, which should not put anybody off, is the inclusion of natural medicinal ingredients used by the Chinese both to enhance flavour and to promote health. These might include ginseng, herbs or dried Himalayan caterpillars.

Another regional favourite is the hot pot (*huoguo*), which is prepared quite differently from its Europeanized version, *fondue chinoise*. In Yunnan, the copper pot, encircling a charcoal-fuelled chimney, was first introduced by Kublai Khan's conquering Mongol army in the 13th century and is probably the authentic, original version. The pot comes to the table already filled with a dozen ingredients simmering in broth—half a dozen vegetables plus miniature meat balls, tiny stuffed omelettes, beancurd in different forms, transparent noodles made from bean flour, and more. Only after the pot is half empty do the diners begin to cook fresh, raw ingredients in the broth. This meal is only eaten in winter and is a marvellously convivial way to spend a cold evening.

Crossing-the-Bridge Rice Noodles (*guoqiao mixian*) is a dish immortalized by a quaint medieval story from southern Yunnan. A scholar, preparing for the imperial examinations, isolated himself on an island in a lake. His devoted wife was dismayed that the meals she carried to him across a long, wooden bridge always arrived cold. But by chance, she discovered the way to keep soup boiling hot was to top it with a thin layer of vegetable oil which prevented the heat from escaping. She was then able to cook thinly sliced meat and vegetables on the spot without a stove. Of course, her husband passed the exams.

Today, by the same technique, diners are presented with a large bowl of scalding broth made from chicken, duck and spareribs, topped by a thin layer of vegetable oil. Numerous side dishes include wafer-thin slices of chicken, liver, fish and pork, green onions, pea-sprouts, Chinese spinach and other seasonal vegetables. Rice noodles, made from rice flour, complete the array. All are quickly put into the broth where, in one bowl, they cook to perfection. This is a light, delicate and highly satisfying meal. The vital elements in the success of Crossing-the-Bridge Rice Noodles are temperature, quality of broth and freshness of the ingredients.

Yunnan is one of China's foremost tea-producing regions and tea is drunk by everybody, usually brewed directly in a large cup with a lid, rather than in a teapot. Green tea of many sorts is the most commonly preferred, though excellent black tea is also available in most hotels. Pu Erh tea, known and beloved in Canton and Hong Kong as *bolei*, is grown and processed in Yunnan.

For beer drinkers, Kunming has its own brewery and also imports beer from other parts of China, especially the well-known Qingdao (Tsingtao) brand, exported world-wide from Shandong Province.

Chinese grape wines, mostly from north China, were once notoriously sweet and syrupy. Recently, the French have helped improve Chinese wine making and the results are sometimes palatable. Rice wines differ from Japanese sake in taste, colour and texture, being generally nuttier, darker and thicker. They are served warm in winter. The Chinese call these wines *huangjiu* (yellow wine) or Shaoxingjiu, whether or not they really originate from the town of Shaoxing in Zhejiang Province.

Strong spirits are usually drunk only by men, especially at banquets and festive occasions. The Chinese call clear, distilled liquor 'white wine' (*baijiu*), which should never be confused with white grape wine (*bai putaojiu*). Beware, for baijiu is white lightning! The best known brand is Maotai, but most Chinese actually prefer Wuliangye, a spirit made from five different grains. These both make a most acceptable gift, and will bring kudos if offered at a banquet.

Shopping

Compared to the markets of Beijing, Shanghai and Canton, Kunming is not a great shopping centre. It does have interesting and unusual items related to the large ethnic minority population, however, and special items deriving from Yunnan's combination of high altitude and southern latitude. Kunming's development as a major regional city means that consumer goods and products, unavailable in the 1980s, are now common.

Kunming's central area is small enough that most shopping can be done on foot or bicycle. The bright clothing and embroidered accessories of Yunnan's minority peoples are favourite purchases. Aprons, shoulder bags, embroidered shoes, head-dresses and belts are particularly attractive. Decorated baby hats, capes, and beautifully appliqued *beibeis* (padded cloth baby carrier, tied to the mother's back) are charming and amusing. Attractive blue and white batik cloth is made up into handbags, dresses, napkins and tablecloths. The Minorities Department Store is the source of many such items as well as cloth, braid, ornaments, buttons and lace. This store also has musical instruments, shoes and boots, caps and knick-knacks. Shops in Kunming's major hotels are also good places to buy minority items, unless you plan to go to the places where the people actually live. Everyday Chinese clothing of cotton or silk makes a good buy—brightly coloured sweat suits, striped T-shirts, corduroy jackets, silk blouses, dress shirts, coats.

Antique shops in Kunming carry mostly porcelains and the usual miscellaneous assortment of chops, snuff bottles, ink stones and wrought silver jewellery. Apart from a lucky find, there is nothing very special here. More fun is to visit the open-air market in the area of Yongdao Jie. Some visitors have been impressed by the jade, which comes mostly from neighbouring Burma. Marble items from Dali can be found everywhere, ranging from finely polished discs with landscapes in the natural grain to heavy, crude flower pots.

Yunnan's special cooking utensils, the ceramic steam pot (*qiguo*) and the copper hot pot (*huoguo*) are handsome and versatile. Other copper items for the kitchen include ladles, bowls, moulds and kettles.

Kunming has several bookshops which are good places to browse for light, inexpensive gifts. The Foreign Language Bookshop has interesting books in English, French, German and other languages on Chinese history, learning Chinese, poetry, contemporary life and children's stories. The large Xinhua Bookshop has colourful posters, maps, art and calligraphy books and calendars.

Many of Yunnan's native products are highly sought after by the Chinese themselves. If you ever need to give a gift or repay a kindness inside China, the following items are thoroughly appropriate. They can also be seen as authentic souvenirs from Southwest China:-

Tea Many varieties of local tea exist; some of the best known names are Pu Erh, Tuo, Dianlu and Dabaicha. Yunnan black tea is also excellent.

Medicines Chinese from all over the world come to Yunnan for its traditional medicines. Some familiarity with the products is necessary for successful shopping, and the mere reading of the packages sends many foreigners reeling. Chinese *angelica*, a herb of the carrot family, is favoured as a pain killer, helps blood circulation and is good for the stomach. Pseudo-ginseng (*sanqi* and *tianqi*) is considered an ideal preventive medicine for cardiovascular disease. *Baiyao* ('white medicine') is a traditional folk remedy made from over 100 kinds of herbs that claims to cure bruises, internal haemorrhaging and gunshot wounds. These are just a few of the pharmacopaeia available.

Cigarettes Most Chinese recognise that the best tobacco in the country comes from Yunnan. The prized brands are Yunyan, Red Camellia, Red Pagoda Mountain and Dazhongjiu.

Food Yunnan ham (Xuanwei *huotui*), either fresh or tinned, is a delicious gift, as are the many types of dried mushrooms.

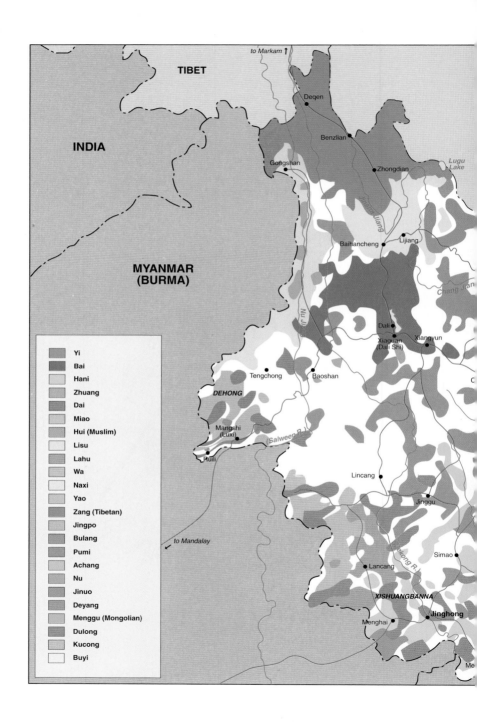

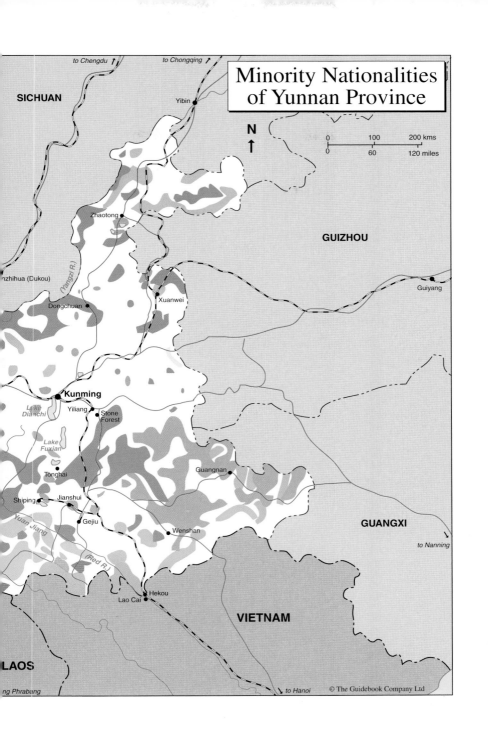

THE MINORITY NATIONALITIES OF YUNNAN

China is a vast country, slightly larger than the United States in surface area, sharing borders with 13 different nations. Its geographical and human make-up is extremely complex; not the mono-dimensional, grey place stereotyped by many outsiders.

The Han Chinese (the name Han comes from China's first long-lasting, unified empire, 206 BC–AD 220) are by far the most important nationality in the country, comprising 94 per cent of the population, but 55 other nationalities, the 'minorities', occupy over 60 per cent of the land mass, much of it in strategic border areas. The Chinese have always realized the significance of these people, who from time to time through the centuries have made their presence known with a vengeance. Barbarian nomads in the north, indefatigable Tibetans in the west and a host of lesser nations on the periphery have chipped away at China whenever it showed vulnerability. Two great dynasties, the Yuan (Mongol) and Qing (Manchu), proved the ascendency of non-Chinese peoples at critical moments in history.

Yunnan is a microcosm of China in the areas of minority affairs and nationality relations. The province has 25 minority groups, nearly half of the country's total. With such ethnic diversity it is important to ask the question: what criteria are used to determine minority status and classification? Basically, there are five ways.

Race
Language
Culture
Religion
History

In Yunnan race is not a major consideration, as it is in northwest China where Caucasian minorities exist. Language and culture, how ever, are of primary interest because they are the basis for classifying most minority nationalities. Religion plays a role in groups such as the Hui (Muslims) who, to all intents and purposes, are Chinese except for their faith. Historical background can sometimes tip the balance in determining the status of a people. The Bai, who have a high cultural level and speak a language closely related to Mandarin, are clearly not Chinese on the basis of their long, well-recorded and independent history.

The linguistic situation in China is very complicated and becomes even more so in Yunnan. Although 700 million Chinese speak Mandarin (putonghua), the national language, and many more speak well-known secondary languages, such as Cantonese and Shanghainese, the babel of minority tongues is impressive and daunting.

Five major language groups exist in China: Sino-Tibetan, Altaic, Austro-Asiatic, Indo-European and Austronesian. Three appear in Yunnan, represented by many smaller language families, of which our knowledge is still incomplete. Some are scarcely known at all and most have not been sufficiently recorded; a main reason for this lacuna was the absence of writing among most minority nationalities. While certain groups did have writing, such as the Bai with their use of Chinese characters, the Hui (Muslims) with their Arabic script, the Naxi with their arcane dongba pictographs and the Tibetans with their alphabet adapted from India, most needed the help of missionaries or contemporary linguists to create a written language.

To the casual observer, the panoply of minority peoples, their peculiar, unfamiliar names, dazzling costumes and wild festivals become little more than an exotic blur. It takes time and effort to differentiate between the groups, to appreciate at a deeper level their special life and unique place among the cultures of the world.

Here is a list of Yunnan Province's minority nationalities. A map showing their geographical distribution is on pages 24–25.

A young lady of the Yi minority

YUNNAN'S MINORITY NATIONALITIES

NAME	POPULATION	LANGUAGE FAMILY
Yi	3,000,000	Tibeto-Burman
Bai	1,050,000	Tibeto-Burman
Hani	930,000	Tibeto-Burman
Zhuang	840,000	Tai
Dai	770,000	Tai
Miao	650,000	Miao-Yao
Hui (Muslim)	400,000	Sinitic
Lisu	325,000	Tibeto-Burman
Lahu	275,000	Tibeto-Burman
Wa	270,000	Mon-Khmer
Naxi	250,000	Tibeto-Burman
Yao	140,000	Miao-Yao
Zang (Tibetan)	90,000	Tibeto-Burman
Jingpo	85,000	Tibeto-Burman
Bulang	55,000	Mon-Khmer
Pumi	22,000	Tai
Buyi	20,000	Tai
Achang	20,000	Tibeto-Burman
Nu	20,000	Tibeto-Burman
Jinuo	12,000	Tibeto-Burman
Deyang	10,000	Mon-Khmer
Sui	9,000	Tai
Menggu (Mongolian)	4,000	Mongol
Dulong	4,000	Tibeto-Burman
Kucong	3,000	Tibeto-Burman

Kunming

Sights in Kunming

YUNNAN PROVINCIAL MUSEUM

Some tourists skip museums on principle, but in this case they really should make an exception. Kunming's museum, housed in a monumental Russian-style building, holds some truly superb cultural treasures. One collection consists of textiles, costumes, handicrafts and artefacts of Yunnan's many ethnic minority groups (see pages 26–28), though the outstanding, priceless assemblage consists of bronzes going back three thousand years (see pages 44–46).

The cavernous ground floor has two wings, to the left and right of the entrance. These hold changing exhibitions of objects from Yunnan's minority cultures. There are few English labels in the entire museum but most of the exhibits speak for themselves. The list below identifies the different groups; upon entering the left wing there is a fine, large map that shows the distribution of Yunnan's various peoples:

1.   The Dai, slender saronged inhabitants of western and southern border regions abutting Laos and Burma, are represented by costumes and textiles from different localities and by musical instruments. Their jewellery includes bangles and enormous silver necklaces.

2.   The Buyi come from the mountainous eastern and southeastern parts of the province. They are similar to the majority Han (largely speaking Chinese and wearing Chinese clothing), though their men sometimes wear head scarves and the women may wear a head scarf, robe and pleated dress for special occasions. Buyi batik work is outstanding.

3.   The Bai are centred around the Dali region, 400 kilometres west of Kunming. They are known for their fine stone and marble work and wood carving. They are the most economically successful of Yunnan's minorities and have been literate in Chinese for centuries.

4.   The Hani from southern Yunnan have various branches; they excel in magnificent jewellery, particularly earrings.

5.   The Achang from the Burmese border are known for their warlike swords and daggers.

6.   The Miao display their batiks and musical instruments, including the wonderful *lu sheng*, a bamboo wind instrument with many projecting pipes. The Miao have resplendent silver jewellery.

7. The Jingpo, scattered through the far west of the province, have large, two-handed swords and intricate jewellery looking like silver armour. They also build tall, coloured pagodas.

8. The Wa, concentrated in remote hills between the Mekong and Salween rivers on the Burmese border, accompany their rituals with drums—bronze and cylindrical wooden drums beautifully painted in red, black and brown.

9. The De'ang live among the western Dai near the Burma border. Their heavy black fabrics are decorated in red and yellow. This minority group is only one of three in China that belong to the Mon-Khmer ethno-linguistic family; the Wa and Bulang are the other two.

10. The Bulang (Blang), closely related to the Wa and De'ang, have been strongly influenced by the Dai. They live in Dai-style bamboo houses, speak Dai as a second language and, when literate, know written Dai. Their polytheism has found a place alongside Theravada Buddhism.

11. The Yi, fourth largest of China's minorities, boast some 30 branches. They have a wide variety of dress. Their ritual life includes the use of masks and clay cat-demons that function as roof tiles.

12. Tibetans (Zang) have resided for centuries in northernmost Yunnan near the Tibetan border. Most adhere to the Yellow Hat (Gelugpa) school of Tibetan Buddhism, and their religious life is centred on a few large monasteries.

13. The Lisu are people of northwestern Yunnan who live in isolated areas near the Salween and Mekong rivers. Many Lisu are Christian.

14. The Naxi from the Lijiang area, within the loop of the Upper Yangzi River (Jinsha Jiang), are one of the few non-Chinese people to have a writing of their own. This rebus-pictographic script, called *dongba wen,* is preserved in small, horizontal booklets and coloured cartoon-like scrolls that depict deities, infernal creatures and natural phenomenon. Other rare artefacts include ritual trumpets, headdresses, wooden plaques and clay figurines.

15. The Pumi (Primi) are spread across northwestern Yunnan. They are known for their colourful costumes and a rich oral tradition. The women especially wear long skirts with bright sashes and sheepskin cloaks. The Pumi are closely related to the Qiang of Sichuan Province and probably migrated from even farther north in the plateau grasslands of Qinghai-Gansu.

16. The Lahu are mountain dwellers, neighbours of the Wa, who use simple agricultural implements.

17. The Jinuo number only 15,000 and live in the rough, mountainous country near the southern Dai.

18. The Muslims (Hui), scattered throughout the province, are considered a minor-

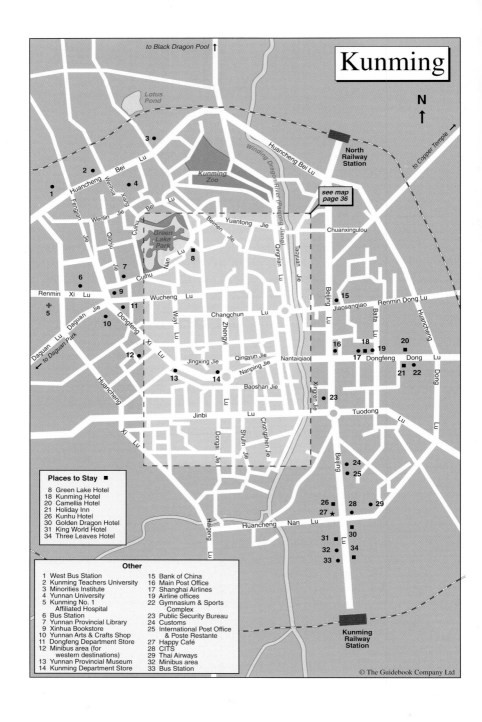

Kunming

N ↑

to Black Dragon Pool ↑

Lotus Pond

to Copper Temple →

North Railway Station

see map page 36

Kunming Zoo

Green Lake Park

Winding Dragon River (Panlong Jiang)

Huancheng Bei Lu

Chuanxingulou

Yuantong Jie

Beimen Jie

Qingnian Lu

Taoyuan Jie

Beijing Lu

Renmin Dong Lu

Jiaosanqiao

Baita Lu

Huancheng Dong Lu

Renmin Xi Lu

Wucheng Lu

Changchun Lu

Zhengyi Lu

Woyi Lu

Qingyun Jie

Nanping Jie

Nantaiqiao

Dongfeng Dong Lu

Jingxing Jie

Baoshan Jie

Xinleng Jie

Tuodong Lu

Dongsi Jie

Shulin Jie

Jinbi Lu

Chongshen Lu

Jinbi Lu

Fengian Jie

Huancheng

Bei Lu

Wenhua Xiang

Wenlin Jie

Olanbu Jie

Daguan Jie

Cuihu Bei Lu

Cuihu Nan Lu

Dongfeng Xi Lu

Daguan Lu

to Daguan Park ←

Huancheng Xi Lu

Haigeng Lu

Huancheng Nan Lu

Beijing Lu

Kunming Railway Station

© The Guidebook Company Ltd

Places to Stay ■

8   Green Lake Hotel
18 Kunming Hotel
20 Camellia Hotel
21 Holiday Inn
26 Kunhu Hotel
30 Golden Dragon Hotel
31 King World Hotel
34 Three Leaves Hotel

Other

1   West Bus Station
2   Kunming Teachers University
3   Minorities Institute
4   Yunnan University
5   Kunming No. 1
      Affiliated Hospital
6   Bus Station
7   Yunnan Provincial Library
9   Xinhua Bookstore
10 Yunnan Arts & Crafts Shop
11 Dongfeng Department Store
12 Minibus area (for
      western destinations)
13 Yunnan Provincial Museum
14 Kunming Department Store

15 Bank of China
16 Main Post Office
17 Shanghai Airlines
19 Airline offices
22 Gymnasium & Sports
      Complex
23 Public Security Bureau
24 Customs
25 International Post Office
      & Poste Restante
27 Happy Café
28 CITS
29 Thai Airways
32 Minibus area
33 Bus Station

ity because of their religion and culture, although physically and linguistically they resemble the majority Han Chinese.

19. The Mongolians (Menggu), remnants of Kublai Khan's conquering army, number only 5,000 and dwell in self-contained villages near Tonghai, in central Yunnan.

20. The Yao are broadly distrubuted over six of China's provinces. In Yunnan they live in the southeasternmost corner and still practice slash-and-burn agriculture. They are often confused with the Miao.

21. The Zhuang are mostly in Guangxi, to the east, where they number more than 12 million, but have sizable communities in southeastern Yunnan as well. They are largely sinicized and speak a language of the Tai family.

22. The Nu live among the wild mountains of northwest Yunnan, along the gorge of the Salween River. The Salween is called Nu in Chinese.

23. Dulung (Drung) people only number five thousand and inhabit the territory where China, Tibet and Burma come together, along the Drung River valley. Women sometimes scar and tatoo their faces, to appear more beautiful, to proclaim they belong to the Dulung and to ward off evil spirits. They practice bull sacrifice.

24. The Sui (Shui) are migrants from Guizhou Province and number only 10,000 in Yunnan out of a total population of nearly 300,000. Bronze drums are an important feature of their culture, which relies on animistic worship of water, trees and stones.

25. The Kucong are a tiny minority group with only 3000 members. They live in southern Yunnan along the border with Vietnam, though some are found farther north in isolated mountainous areas. They are not officially recognized as a separate minority; some say they are related to the Hani, others to the Lahu.

On the museum's upper floor, two halls are devoted entirely to Yunnan's archaeology, most notably the famous bronzes (see pages 44–46). Four major Bronze-Age sites have been excavated since 1955. Shizhaishan, at the southern tip of Lake Dianchi, and Jiangchuan,100 kilometres (63 miles) south of Kunming, were at the heart of an ancient kingdom named Dian which flourished from 1100 BC until the first century BC. Chuxiong, 185 kilometres (116 miles), and Xiangyun, 340 kilometres (212 miles) west of Kunming, were home to a western branch of the Dian culture. Their art was less refined and used less decoration than the masterpieces found in tombs at Shizhaishan and Jiangchuan. Dian artisans were among the first people in the world to cast metal by the lost wax method. A clear model of a bronze drum being cast by this method is displayed at the centre of the exhibition.

Long-horned, high-humped cattle played a central role in Dian culture. A measure of wealth, the beasts were only used for sacrifice, never for agriculture. A beautiful use of the ox motif in art can be seen on a bronze sacrificial table. The head, chest and forelegs of the powerful animal form one end; the flat table surface represents its back; its upturned tail and hind quarters are being attacked by an acrobatic tiger. A smallhorned calf, appearing crosswise under the table, completes the composition. Function, concept and craftsmanship blend to meet the needs of a sacrificial ceremony. In another display case, an elegant bronze headrest uses ox heads for its raised points while cattle and horses in light relief decorate its base.

The most intriguing exhibits reveal details of life on the Yunnan plain three thousand years ago. The lids of giant cowrie holders become circular arenas on which figurines play out various vivid scenes. Cowrie holders were essentially treasuries, containing the cowrie shells that served as currency throughout Southeast Asia. (Cowries continued to be used as money in Yunnan until the early 20th century and the shells can still be seen sewn into the headdresses of minority costumes.)

The scenes depict hand-to-hand battles, ceremonial tribute-payment, head-hunting expeditions, a slave-owner overseeing women weavers, and all sorts of daily actions that draw one intimately into a distant way of life. Some of the figurines have large, Caucasoid noses, round eyes, beards and heavy clothing, raising the possibility of early migrations from Central Asia. The details are wonderful and they tell much about the material and philosophical world of the Dian.

One elaborate piece shows an altar at which two slave-owners are consecrating an alliance. To the left and right of the altar, cattle are being slaughtered to strains of music. Tigers and horses are being fed. Behind the altar, a human sacrifice is in progress. Though rich and crowded, the whole configuration is a masterpiece of balanced symmetry.

Bronze drums form a whole category of their own. Some are immense in size, beautifully decorated in relief, with stylized frogs as handles. The earliest bronze drum in the world, dating from the sixth century BC, was found in Yunnan. Members of the Wa and Sui minorities use bronze drums to this day, as do tribal people elsewhere in Southeast Asia.

Some of the most impressive objects in the exhibition are small statues of animals. Their meticulous, forceful realism has rarely been surpassed in any age. This author's favourites are a peacock with a snake in its mouth, two tigers attacking a boar, a wild duck catching fish and two bulls in mortal struggle. An ensemble showing a wolf and a leopard fighting over a disembowelled deer is filled with emotion and pathos and awakens in one nature's awesome power.

On a lighter note, do not miss the outrageous little pas de deux performed by two drunkards. Dancing barefoot on a snake, with swords at their sides, they sing and shout while balancing cymbals, or perhaps shallow bowls, on their palms.

Other displays at the provincial museum include photographs of Yunnan and Kunming. One particularly illuminating exhibition shows the work of Bert Krezyk, an American from Wisconsin, who was a war photographer in the 1940s. His black-and-white pictures capture the special flavour of Yunnan life half a century ago.

YUANTONG TEMPLE (YUANTONGSI), PARK AND ZOO

The well-restored, thousand-year-old Buddhist temple lies in the north part of the city at the foot of Yuantong Hill. Its elaborate entrance is on Yuantong Jie and the impressive gateway dates from the Ming Dynasty.

The temple was founded in the eighth century, when Yunnan was an independent kingdom adjacent to Tang Dynasty China. The whole complex was greatly enlarged in 1320 after the conquest of southwest China (1253) by the Mongol Kublai Khan. For centuries it remained the largest Buddhist monastery in Kunming. Today, Yuantong Temple consists of a Great Hall of the Buddha, the Octagonal Pavilion and garden-like walkways around a pond. In 1990 a Thai-style temple was built behind the main hall to accommodate the large number of Thai tourists in Yunnan, and a small Tibetan chapel on the east side rounds out the complex's Buddhist ecumenism.

Legend says the temple and monastery were first built to control a malicious dragon who lived in a small pond behind the present buildings. Two huge pillars inside the Great Hall are adorned with carved dragons, reminders of their ancient ancestor.

One of the pleasures of Yuantong Temple is to enjoy a cup of green tea among ornamental plants beside the pond, and breathe in the atmosphere of old China. Centuries-old poems are inscribed on the rocky hillside as you look up towards the park and zoo.

Yuantong Park's main entrance lies at the end of Qingnian Lu by the bus terminal. The park, spreading over the slopes of Yuantong Hill, is famous for its flowers and trees. Four main gardens exhibit exquisite blossoms at different times of the year. In summer, many varieties of Yunnan's celebrated rhododendrons are on display. Autumn brings a riot of variegated chrysanthemums. Throughout Kunming's pleasant winter there comes a succession of magnolia, cassia, flowering plum and camellia. The best display of all occurs in late February and March when avenues of Japanese and Oriental cherry create a fairyland of delicate colour.

Kunming's zoo forms the western part of Yuantong Park. Many of Yunnan's

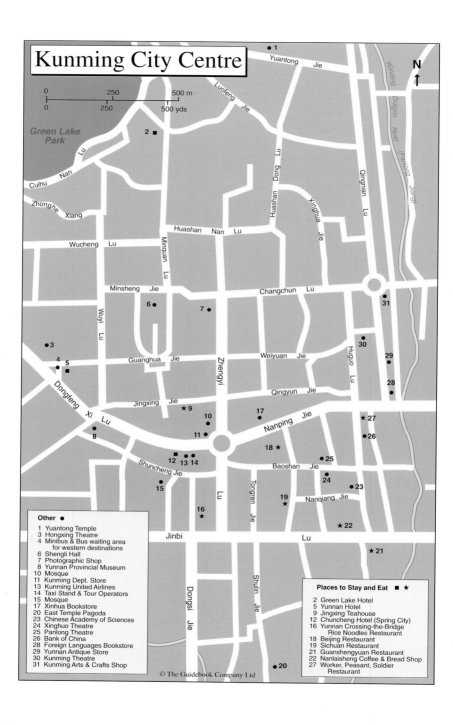

Kunming City Centre

N

Green Lake
Park

0   250   500 m
0   250   500 yds

Yuantong   Jie   • 1

Luofeng   Jie

Lu

Cuihu

Nan

Zhonghe

Xiang

Dong   Lu

Huashan

Qingnian   Lu

Xinghua   Jie

2 ■

Wucheng   Lu

Huashan   Nan   Lu

Minquan   Lu

Minsheng   Jie

Changchun   Lu

31

Wuyi   Lu

6 •

7 •

• 3

30

29

Guanghua   Jie

Weiyuan   Jie

Huguo   Lu

4
5 ■

Zhengyi

Qingyun   Jie

28

Dongfeng

Jingxing   Jie

★ 9

10

17 •

Nanping   Jie

★ 27

Xi   Lu

11 •

• 26

8 •

18 ★

12 ■
13 • 14 •

Baoshan   Jie

25 •

Shuncheng   Jie

24 •

• 23

15 •

16 ★

Lu

Tongren   Jie

19 ★

Nanqiang   Jie

★ 22

Jinbi

Lu

★ 21

Dongsi   Jie

Shulin   Jie

• 20

Winding   Dragon   River   (Panlong   Jiang)

© The Guidebook Company Ltd

Other ●

1   Yuantong Temple
3   Hongxing Theatre
4   Minibus & Bus waiting area
     for western destinations
6   Shengli Hall
7   Photographic Shop
8   Yunnan Provincial Museum
10   Mosque
11   Kunming Dept. Store
13   Kunming United Airlines
14   Taxi Stand & Tour Operators
15   Mosque
17   Xinhua Bookstore
20   East Temple Pagoda
23   Chinese Academy of Sciences
24   Xinghuo Theatre
25   Panlong Theatre
26   Bank of China
28   Foreign Languages Bookstore
29   Yunnan Antique Store
30   Kunming Theatre
31   Kunming Arts & Crafts Shop

Places to Stay and Eat ■ ★

2   Green Lake Hotel
5   Yunnan Hotel
9   Jingxing Teahouse
12   Chuncheng Hotel (Spring City)
16   Yunnan Crossing-the-Bridge
     Rice Noodles Restaurant
18   Beijing Restaurant
19   Sichuan Restaurant
21   Guanshengyuan Restaurant
22   Nanlaisheng Coffee & Bread Shop
27   Worker, Peasant, Soldier
     Restaurant

indigenous species are found here, including wild oxen, peacocks, elephants, tigers, and the handsome, red, raccoon-like lesser panda—as well as the obligatory giant panda from Sichuan Province. All Chinese zoos are a bit sad.

EAST AND WEST TEMPLE PAGODAS (DONGSI TA, XISI TA)

South of Jinbi Lu stand two ancient pagodas, the oldest surviving structures in Kunming. As historical and architectural monuments they are invaluable though they may seem insignificant or run-down at first glance. Both pagodas were constructed in the first half of the ninth century, by a famous artisan named Weichi Chingde, and display marvelous skill in engineering

The 13-tiered pagoda rising 40.5 metres (133 feet) above Shulin Jie is known by three different names: East Temple Pagoda, Golden Chicken Pagoda (Jinji Ta, the popular name, designating four golden roosters on its summit) and Changle Temple Pagoda (the scholarly name, denoting a temple that once surrounded the site). The dilapidated, wild chickens are still there, made of copper rather than gold. The solid base, eight metres tall, is abutted on the right by a lovely series of semi-circular stairs. An important Qing-Dynasty stele at the base describes the history of the two pagodas and their many renovations.

The West Temple Pagoda, also with 13 tiers, is slightly shorter, squatter, and better preserved than its twin, though it lacks the ancient grandeur of East Temple Pagoda. It stands 35.5 metres (116 feet) tall within a small park where old folks drink tea and play mahjong. Reach it by going down a long alleyway west from Dongsi Jie.

INCANTATION PILLAR (DIZANG SI JING CHUANG)

This important 12th-century carved pillar is difficult to find. It stands in a secluded, run-down garden inside the compound of the Cultural Relics Administration at 120 Tuodong Lu in the southeast part of Kunming. Pass from the street through a gateway, then down a driveway straight ahead along a white wall to a second gateway, beyond which stands the pillar. The staff may try to prevent you from entering the garden and seeing it. If this happens, try to see the officer in charge, in a small office nearby, and explain that you have come from the other side of the world to visit this sight.

And the struggle is worth it. Here on a dais stands an octagonal stone pillar carved effusively with 262 images. It is 6.73 metres (20 feet) tall and rises in a succession of different sections. At the base is a round drum carved with four pairs of dragons. Above is an octagonal platform inscribed entirely with Chinese characters that recount sections of sutras and record the builders and sponsors of the pillar.

Here, too, is the approximate date of construction during the Dali Kingdom (937–1253). Next is the largest section, which presents the Guardians of the Four Directions (Four Guardian Kings). These are beautifully sculpted; an exceptional figure is Vaisravana, shown standing on a mother goddess holding a staff. He is executed in the style of Khotan, an important centre of the Silk Road in Xinjiang, and differs from the other three guardians. Look for the bird on his headdress. All four figures are backed by Buddhist scriptures carved in Brahmi script.

Tapering upward are five more sections, or registers, the top two supported by a round vase. These are copiously carved with Buddhas, bodhisattvas, guardians, offertory figures, disciples and celestial beings. The iconography is complex and crowded, though clearly part of the pillar's overall precise and planned configuration.

The Inscription Pillar appears to be a visual summing up of the particular form of Esoteric Buddhism that existed in western Yunnan during the late Dali Kingdom.

CONFUCIAN TEMPLE

The Ming-Dynasty Confucian Temple (Wen Miao) stands inside the grounds of the Yishu Juyuan (Art Theatre) along Wen Miao Jie, one of the last small streets in Kunming to retain its old flavour and charm. The temple itself is known for the outstanding eaves and latticework entranceway. The latter dates from the late 17th century.

GREEN LAKE PARK (CUIHU GONGYUAN)

This lively, attractive park lies in the northwestern quarter of the city. Originally a marsh on the outskirts of Kunming, it was transformed into a park in the late 17th century under Emperor Kangxi; his servants drained the swamp, put in the lake, built the main pavilion and installed the causeways and arbours.

In the early morning the park hums with traditional Chinese life: elderly gentlemen practising martial arts or airing their pet birds, children exercising, old women gossiping. The park is a gathering place for singers who have revived long-dormant folk songs and operas. Everybody enjoys the open-air performances at any time of day, but most frequently on weekends. Green Lake Park is especially colourful on festival days, such as Mid-Autumn Festival or Chinese New Year.

MOSQUES (QINGZHENSI)

At least five mosques serve Kunming's 40,000-strong Muslim population. The two main ones welcome visitors who behave in a modest and circumspect manner. The oldest and leading mosque of the city is located adjacent to the Central Department Store at 51 Zhengyi Lu. It is some 400 years old and noted for its murals depicting the holy Islamic sites of Mecca and Medina.

A larger mosque is situated down a white-washed alley that leaves the main road at 90 Shuncheng Jie, in the centre of the city's Muslim quarter, not far from the Yunnan Provincial Museum. Quaint shops and halal restaurants specializing in beef and lamb dishes cater to Muslims in the neighbourhood. The well-preserved mosque is an interesting mixture of Chinese and Arabian styles. A large prayer hall with an elaborate roof faces an open courtyard where the white-clad worshippers come streaming through after daily prayers, especially on Fridays.

WALKING OR BICYCLING IN TOWN

A walk or a bike ride through Kunming is easy and fun. In spite of a population of two million, the main part of the city is compact, about 4 kilometres (2.5 miles) in diameter, encircled by a ring road, Huancheng Lu. Street names are posted in pinyin romanization as well as Chinese characters, so it is easy to follow a map.

A visitor's first impression of the city is often of broad, modern avenues flanked by grey, featureless buildings, and indeed, over the past decade Kunming has grown from a little, manageable city to an important, overcrowded regional centre, with all the problems of a modern Asian metropolis. Nevertheless, a view from the top of the Kunming Hotel or Green Lake Hotel will show that such arteries merely form a wide grid placed over the ancient city, and that some of the spaces between them are filled with crooked lanes, low wooden houses with tiled roofs and carved upper storeys, craftsmen's shops, teahouses, little courtyards and tiny gardens. Though constantly under attack by builders and modernizers, these interstices continue to exist with the life and flavour of traditional China.

• A WALK FROM THE KUNMING HOTEL (ONE AND HALF HOURS)

At the hotel gate, turn right (west) on Dongfeng Dong Lu, Kunming's main avenue, and walk for two long blocks to the main square. Cross the square diagonally towards the southwest corner. The square itself is full of activity at most times of the day and evening—*taijiquan* (tai ch'i) and martial arts are practised in the morning; kite-flying, domino games and street stalls occupy it in the afternoon; a cross-section of the city promenades through it in the evening. When you reach the Winding Dragon River (Panlong Jiang), turn left and follow the small lane southward along its bank to Jinbi Lu. Picturesque scenes flank the riverbank. Jinbi Lu's character comes from its role, in former times, as the commercial centre of Kunming's Vietnamese and Cantonese communities. Tinkers, box-makers, scroll-mounters and artisans are juxtaposed with bakeries, tiny sweet shops and coffee shops. Turn right on Jinbi Lu and walk westward for about five blocks to Tongren

(Following pages) *The Road to Deqen*

Jie. Turn right down this charming arcaded street to its end at Baoshan Jie. Turn right, and continue for about five blocks past a variety of shops and theatres to Huguo Lu, where a left turn will bring you quickly back to Dongfeng Dong Lu. The square is on your right, and the Kunming Hotel is two blocks beyond that.

• A WALK FROM THE GREEN LAKE HOTEL (ONE AND A HALF HOURS)
The hotel stands opposite Green Lake Park, which makes an enjoyable excursion in itself, but for a fuller appreciation of Kunming's old charm, you need to strike out into the neighbouring streets and alleys.

Leaving the main gate of the hotel's old wing, not the new high-rise, turn left sharply and follow the small flagstoned street for two minutes to a gateway on your left guarded by two stone lions. The gateway and lions marked a curious old temple, now gone; inside the courtyard is a primary school. Continue straight along the flagstoned lane until it rejoins Cuihu Nan Lu, the road which encircles Green Lake Park, and then bear left for about 300 metres.

Turn left on Honghua Qiao until it reaches the distinct main street called Wucheng Lu, ascending a hill to the left. This bustling thoroughfare is an agglomeration of eccentric shops selling spectacles, alarm clocks, wine, cloth, noodles, office safes and firecrackers, among other things. At the top of the hill Wucheng Lu ends at Minquan Jie; turn right here. Minquan Jie leads for about half a kilometre through a quiet, old residential area. The road veers to the right at the bottom of the hill and joins a main intersection. Straight ahead is an extraordinary, narrow building, and on the right a huge flight of stone steps—a favourite haunt of naughty schoolboys who sometimes shoot down the stairway riding their mothers' washboards.

From the steps, cross the main thoroughfare, Guanghua Jie, and work your way into the amazing street market that runs south along Yongdao Jie, a little, arboured street overflowing with everything old and precious in Kunming, from potted plants, bonsai and antiques to birds, lacquerware and musical instruments. After one block it reaches Jingxing Jie. To your left is a famous teashop, rarely noticed by tourists, where traditional bards tell stories to enraptured audiences of old men. After a cup of tea, backtrack along Jingxing Jie to its end at Wuyi Lu. Turn right and continue straight north until you finally reach Green Lake Park. Turn right on Cuihu Nan Lu and you will see the hotel ahead.

UNIVERSITY QUARTER
Four institutions of higher education lie on Kunming's northwest edge beyond Green Lake Park. The campuses flank Huancheng Bei Lu near the Western Station (Xi Zhan) interchange. Formal arrangements to visit any of the institutions can be

made through CITS or the schools themselves. However, you may just want to stroll through the university quarter and chat with students informally.

Farthest east is the Yunnan Institute for Nationalities, easily recognized by its large, conspicuous entrance gate. Known colloquially as the Minorities Institute, the campus was set up in 1951 as a training school for political cadres from Yunnan's many ethnic groups. Today the institute offers a broad curriculum to 1,500 students representing all of Yunnan's minority peoples.

A few steps to the west, straddling Huancheng Bei Lu, is Yunnan University, the largest and most important of the four institutions. Established privately in 1923 as Eastern Continental University, it had evolved into a fully-fledged provincial university by the mid-1930s. After the 1949 revolution, specialized colleges such as agriculture, medicine and engineering were split off and established as independent schools. The remaining faculties of arts and sciences now boast 10,000 of Yunnan's brightest students. A walk through the tree-lined campus reveals the architectural history of the university, from the old French-style administration building to the recently added departments of law and economics.

Directly behind Yunnan University lies Kunming Engineering College. Its large campus peters out in the new suburbs and red hills north of Kunming.

Just west of Yunnan University, on Huancheng Bei Lu, lies Kunming Teachers University, which vies with Yunnan University in size and status. Its function is to provide high quality teachers for Yunnan Province's educational system. From 1938 to 1946, this site was occupied by the Southwest Associated University, an institution that played a vital role in modern China's social, intellectual and political history. Refugee teachers and students from universities in Beijing and Tianjin fled across China, pulling their libraries in carts, to escape the invading Japanese. They gathered in Kunming, where they kept alive the flame of free learning throughout the war.

TANHUA TEMPLE AND PARK

In the eastern part of the city, off Renmin Dong Lu, beyond the railway tracks, is Tanhua Temple and its grounds, which have been turned into a park and Buddhist amusement centre.

The temple buildings are worth seeing. They retain the essential style of the original structures, built in 1634 in the closing years of the Ming Dynasty, though many reconstructions have taken place since then. The temple complex has for more than 300 years been synonymous with Kunming and its love of flowers and gardens. Within living memory, the abbot Yingding (died 1922), a brilliant Buddhist and Confucian scholar, was recognized for his gardening skills; he revitalized the grounds.

THE BRONZES OF YUNNAN

Bronze art seems to arise almost spontaneously in China. As more discoveries are made and the location of sites increases, the possibility of independent development increases as well.

The discovery in Yunnan of magnificent bronze artwork from the dawn of history excited archaeologists around the world. Farmers ploughing near Lake Dianchi unearthed some mystifying bronze vessels in the early 1950s and notified the provincial museum in Kunming. In 1955, archaeologists struck a treasure trove of 48 Bronze-Age tombs at Stone Village Hill (Shizhaishan), 40 kilometres (25 miles) south of Kunming.

Bronze is an alloy of copper and tin which is stronger than iron if made in correct proportions—eight parts copper to one part tin. Bronze was the first metal ever used by humans. It first came into use in northern China during the Shang Dynasty, around 1800 BC. Yunnan's bronze culture dates from about 1200 BC, near the end of the Shang Dynasty, though most of the bronze artifacts from the 48 tombs date from the Warring States Period (475–221 BC) and the Western Han Dynasty (206 BC–AD 24).

The Dian people in Yunnan mastered many advanced techniques in creating their bronzes, including gold plating and silver inlay decorations. Skill and sophistication of workmanship equalled and surpassed that of the Han. And whereas Han bronze culture seemed to undergo a change in favour or porcelain, the Dian bronzes took on new confidence and variety. Free from the constraints of orthodoxy, the Dian artists could create more freely and respond to the calling of their aesthetic choice. One can even say that 'art for art's sake' was being created in Southwest China at that time.

The tombs at Shizhaishan yielded thousands of bronze objects—

sewing boxes, figurines, headrests, mirrors, weapons, farm implements, belt buckles and more. Animals, hunting and fighting, took a predominant place among the statuettes and decorations. Archaeologists found 34 recognizable species along with many mythological beasts. Subsequent digs in western Yunnan produced a little bronze house with six kinds of domesticated animals—cow, goat, chicken, dog, pig, horse—pointing to an advanced agricultural society.

Even more revealing were elaborate, three-dimensional scenes cast on the lids of huge cowrie containers and on drums, showing the daily life of a vigorous, productive, slave-owning people. To archaeologists, this was a unique moment in the history of bronzeware. Only in Yunnan did Bronze-Age artisans realistically record the intimate and unmistakable details of their social activity. There were ferocious miniature battles and lively domestic scenes showing the work of women. The rhythms and rituals of agriculture and religion came to life, along with grisly depictions of head-hunting and human sacrifice. The bronze figurines laughed, wept, got drunk. One scene showed pompously dressed chieftains, surrounded by slaves, offering tribute to the King of Dian. Who were these people?

The first historical reference to the Kingdom of Dian appears in the second century BC. Sima Qian (145–85 BC), China's greatest classical historian, mentions that the King of Dian, in the savage southern border region beyond China, allied himself with the emperor of the Han Dynasty in order to subdue neighbouring tribes. In recognition of Dian's new tributary status, a seal was presented to the King of Dian. Other references to Dian appeared here and there in ancient Chinese literature but there was no hard evidence to confirm the kingdom's existence until 1956. That year, tomb Number 6 at Shizhaishan yielded up the seal itself. Four clear characters on its bronze face—Dian Wang Zhi Yin

(Seal of the King of Dian)—bound this remote, remarkable tribe to the vast empire of China.

Dian originally referred only to the mysterious, non-Chinese tribe. Later the name came to mean the territorial kingdom as well. The Lake of Dian (Dianchi) outside Kunming has kept its ancestral name for three millennia and the word Dian remains synonymous with Yunnan.

On the basis of available material, archaeologists divide Yunnanese bronze age culture into four categories, according to geography. Dianchi culture, Erhai culture (in the area around Dali and Erhai Lake), Northwest Yunnan culture and Yuanjiang culture (or Red River culture, in southern Yunnan). The most important Dianchi culture is concentrated around Lake Dianchi outside Kunming, but extends to Qujing in the northeast, to the Red River in the south, Luling County in the east and Lufung County in the west.

A major element in the bronze culture of Yunnan is the bull, symbol of property and wealth. The depictions of the beast are powerful and realistic, where even the veins on the head and neck stand out. The tiger, too, appears again and again as a creature of strength and awe, holding forth the aspiration of invincibility.

Ancestor worship is clearly presented in the bronze work of Dian. In some cases there is presented a beautiful house-shrine with a snake-staircase that leads to a roof. It is designed to reach ever upward and to lead the eye that way. A figure with hair braided upward mirrors the stairway. The visual story seems to say: The Dian people can reach to Heaven to communicate with their ancestors by means of the snake ladder; the spirit of the snake stands as an intermediary between the world of men and the celestial world.

'Tanhua' is the Chinese name for the broad-leaved epiphyllum (*Epiphyllum oxypetalum*), which produces a large, beautiful and fragrant white flower that opens only briefly, sometimes for just one night, before dying. The Chinese phrase *tanhua yixian* means to flower as briefly as the epiphyllum, and thus describes anything wonderful, fragile and transitory.

Sights near Kunming

WESTERN HILL (XISHAN)

The name Western Hill refers to a range of four mountains stretching over 40 kilometres (25 miles) along the western shore of Lake Dianchi. Seen from a distance, its skyline resembles a Sleeping Beauty with long tresses trailing away to the south. It offers the best scenery and some of the finest temples in the entire region. Its highest temple, Dragon Gate, is nearly 2,500 metres (8,200 feet) high.

Western Hill affords four major attractions. On the lower and middle slopes are two important Buddhist temples. On the steep, higher reaches are a Daoist temple, grottoes and a superb view across the lake and the whole Yunnan plain from the Dragon Gate itself.

From the bus stop at Gao Qiao Station at the mountain's base, a walk of 2.5 kilometres (1.5 miles) along the road brings you to Huating Temple (Huating Si), the largest Buddhist complex in Kunming. A grand garden at the entrance includes an ornamental lake surrrounded by a wall with three-metre (ten-foot) high white stupas. These small towers, whose shape derives from ancient burial mounds, are the fundamental symbol of Buddhism. Two wrathful deities, known as Heng (with mouth closed) and Ha (mouth open), stand at the temple entrance. Coloured with lacquer, they are considered to be among the best representations of these celestial guardians in all China. Inside the entrance hall are even larger statues of the Kings of the Four Directions, dressed in the splendid armour of Chinese warriors a thousand years ago, before Mongol and Manchu invasions introduced alien martial regalia.

Earliest references to Huating go back to the 11th century. An important monastery in the 14th century, it continued to grow and reached its present dimensions only in 1420. Today, there are 40 monks in residence and renovated quarters can accommodate pilgrims and visitors.

The main temple contains a trinity of gilded lacquer Buddhas seated on lotus thrones. Their huge size, blue hair, and sumptuous setting make an impressive sight. The side walls are covered with a phantasmagoria of folk characters—these

are the same 500 *luohan* (holy men, spiritual adepts and disciples of the Buddha) as the ones in the Bamboo Temple (see page 51)—made deliberately comical to contrast with the calm solemnity of the great Buddhas. One, on stilt-like legs, grabs for the moon; another has eyebrows reaching to his knees.

Behind the three Buddhas, facing the back of the hall, is a shrine to Guanyin, the Goddess of Mercy. Against an elaborate backdrop, a kind of mythological bestiary, she rides across the sea on a dragon's head to meet the Dragon King, who waits for her on the left.

Leaving Huating, follow the main road up the mountain for 2 kilometres (1.25 miles) to a secondary road leading sharply off to the right. A short walk brings you to Taihua Temple (Taihua Si), which many people feel is aesthetically superior to the larger complex below. Nestled in a deep forest, Taihua's site is one of its charms. Age-old camellia and magnolia trees give shade in a meticulously cultivated garden. The top level at the back offers a stunning view over temple roofs to the lake far below. The mossy, upturned eaves, the ancient, gnarled trees and the square-rigged fishing boats dotting the lake could have emerged from a traditional scroll painting. A visit to this Buddhist retreat in the late afternoon or the cool of the evening, when the crowds have gone, can transport you to another century, far removed from modern China.

At the entrance, a handsome stone archway is covered with fine carvings: Buddhist symbols, flowers and creatures, including an animated cockatoo. In the Four Guardians entrance hall beyond, an image of Guanyin replaces the usual fat, merry Buddha, as Taihua is dedicated to the Goddess of Mercy.

The main temple building bears the name Hall of the Precious Hero, in honour of a statue near the back representing Zishi, the Daoist hero-god of the Copper Temple (see page 55). His prominent place in a temple of a different religion is explained by his local popularity and the eclectic nature of Buddhism in China. Behind the temple's trinity of Buddhas and a high, finely worked wooden pavilion, stands an altar to Guanyin, facing the rear. Here Yunnan's favourite goddess fulfills her role as Deliverer of Sons, holding out an unmistakably male baby to newlyweds and barren couples. Beside her stand Zishi, the Daoist, and Wen Cheng (Sanskrit: Manjushri), God of Wisdom and Literature, clad in yellow. These two anticipate the shrines awaiting on the final stretch of the mountainside.

A 2-kilometre (1.25-mile) walk brings you to the end of the paved road and the climax of Western Hill, Sanqing Pavilion (Sanqing Ge) and the Dragon Gate (Longmen). Halfway along, a short distance to the right, lies an old cemetery with many traditional tombs and gravestones. A late addition contains the ashes of Nie Er, the brilliant young musician who composed China's present national anthem. He was tragically drowned in Japan in 1936 at the age of 24.

At the end of the road, a long flight of steps ascends to the Pavilion of the Three Pure Ones (Sanqing Ge), a collection of almost vertical buildings stacked against the face of the mountain. Unfortunately, little is left in their interiors except for the central Sanqing pavilion, where three statues of Zishi present him as a black-faced heavenly potentate as well as the familiar warrior god.

Sanqing was originally built in the early 14th century as a summer resort for a Mongol prince of the Yuan Dynasty. Renovated 400 years later as a Daoist shrine, it now contains a large teahouse with a splendid view and gives a welcome pause before the final climb.

A stone path leads up past a series of caves and grottoes to the Air Corridor, a tunnel chipped out of living rock. At the far end, it opens out through a stone archway to a temple eyrie on the side of a sheer cliff. The characters *longmen* (dragon gate) are inscribed in red and gold upon the arch.

In the year 1781, an impoverished Daoist monk named Wu Laiqing from Sanqing Pavilion began chipping his way up the cliff with hammer and chisel, motivated by devotion. After his death, two pious gentlemen from the region continued his project, aided by villagers from the foot of the mountain. Working day and night in rain or shine, hanging from ropes, they inched the route precariously upward to a natural cliff-top platform, completing Wu Laiqing's visionary plan in 1853. The view from the final terrace is excellent and worth the walk.

A shrine in the rock wall, called Attainment of Heaven Cave, holds the lively golden image of Kui Xing, patron god of scholars. He rides a dragon-fish while heroically brandishing a calligraphy brush—as though to confirm that the pen is mightier than the sword—and blithely balances a potted pomegranate plant, the symbol of long-lasting success, on the sole of his foot. Candidates for the all-important imperial examinations struggled up Western Hill to pray for his help. He is flanked by Wen Cheng, the God of Wisdom and Literature, and Guan Gong, the God of War and Justice. Symbols of bounty, happiness and longevity surround the trio. Cranes and peaches, representing long life, adorn the ceiling. Phoenixes and peacocks, chess-boards and horses, stand for power and intellectual pleasure. Coloured clouds represent happiness and prosperity. High above the cave, the stone head of a benign old man peers down from a niche. He is none other than Laozi (Lao-Tse), the founder of Daoism.

This particular gathering of gods, sages and emblems symbolized the ambitions of candidates aspiring to high office in the imperial bureaucracy or the army. Successful scholars have left grateful poems and inscriptions along the route above Sanqing. A few failed candidates leapt to their death in despair from the top of Dragon Gate.

An alternative route back to Kunming from the Western Hill follows a steep path straight down the mountain. It starts from the paved road close to Sanqing Ge and comes out at Dragon Gate Village (Longmen Cun) at the base. From here you can see a long, narrow causeway extending out into Lake Dianchi. Go to its end, where you will find a ferry consisting of a wooden boat punted by the cheerful womenfolk of a local peasant family. Upon landing after a five-minute ride, walk east on a clearly marked path by the water's edge to the resort village of Haigeng (see page 58), where you can catch a bus back to Kunming, 10 kilometres away.

DAGUAN PARK (DAGUAN GONGYUAN)

This large, lake-filled park lies 3 kilometres (1.8 miles) southwest of Kunming at the end of the Number 4 bus line. Built in 1690 under Emperor Kangxi, its rambling, willowed causeways and hump-backed bridges all centre on Daguan Pavilion. Daguan means 'grand view'. True to its name, the three-storey pavilion provides a spectacular view across sparkling Lake Dianchi to the distant Western Hill.

On the pavilion's lakeside facade, two long inscriptions flank a false entranceway, forming a single poem. Written by Sun Ranweng, a famous Qing-Dynasty scholar, this great couplet of 180 characters is one of Yunnan Province's most valued cultural treasures. The first half, on the right, praises the beautiful scenery around Kunming, characterizing local mountains and extolling nature in a sunny, optimistic mood. The second half, on the left, traces 2000 years of Yunnan's history, commemorating its rulers and warriors, battles and victories. It ends, however, on a melancholy, philosophical note.

> *Where are they now?. . . neither the setting sun nor the rising fog casts a glance at the crumbling monuments and dilapidated tombstones. What alone remains through eternity are the twinkling lights of the fishermen's boats, the lines of wild geese in the calm autumnal sky, the ringing bell of a distant monastery and the frost that stealthily sets upon the lake's shore.*

BAMBOO TEMPLE (QIONGZHU SI)

On the wooded slopes of Yu'an Hill, 12 kilometres (7.5 miles) northwest of Kunming, stands this author's favourite temple. The Bamboo Temple offers the best introduction to Buddhist art and architecture in the region because of its completeness and relative simplicity.

Legend tells that two princes went hunting in the hills outside Kunming in the

BASIC FORMAT OF TEMPLES

In spite of variations in size, detail and topography, most temples in Yunnan follow the same layout. An entrance hall leads in to an open courtyard bounded on the sides by monastic living quarters and galleries. The main temple stands at the rear with one or two additional temple buildings behind it. The temple usually faces south with the entrance at the lowest level, flanked by two guardian figures, either animal or demonic.

The entrance hall usually contains a fat, laughing Buddha and four giant kings, guardians of the four directions. East is white, and he carries a lute. South is blue, and he carries a sword. West is red, and he carries a pagoda or a pearl. North is orange, and he carries a stylized Buddhist banner. The chief of the Four Kings is East.

Courtyards vary greatly, depending on the site, but they commonly hold ancient, sacred trees, a garden and sometimes a pool or fountain.

The main temple normally has central statues of three aspects of the Buddha, or of a single Buddha and two of his disciples. They may be attended by any number of figures representing bodhisattvas, disciples and mythological beings. Behind the main statues there is often a shrine to Guanyin, the Chinese Godess of Mercy.

The second or third temple building often gives access to a confusing maze of outbuildings, small courtyards, vegetable gardens and so on.

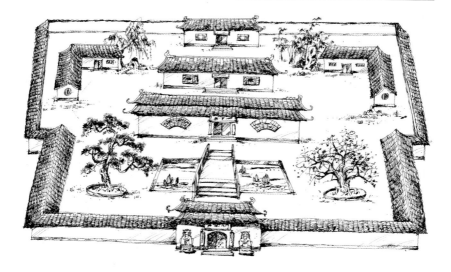

Temple guardian from the Huating temple complex, Western Hill (Xishan)

year 638. A magical rhinoceros led them deep into a forest where it suddenly disappeared. In its stead emerged a group of strange-looking monks carrying staves of bamboo. They too vanished in a purple cloud, but not before leaving their walking sticks planted in the ground. These promptly sprouted leaves and within a day had become an entire grove of special *qiong* bamboo. Here the devout brothers founded a Buddhist temple to honour the miraculous encounter. In fact, the temple, representing the Chan (Zen) sect, has been destroyed and rebuilt many times. The present dimensions seem to date from around 1280, during the reign of Kublai Khan.

The monastery stands on a high stone terrace made from the foundations of earlier temples. A narrow forecourt holds two majestic 450-year old cypress trees. The entrance hall contains statues of the Four Guardian Kings. On the right of the main courtyard reside the Bamboo Temple's best known attractions—500 finely crafted, idiosyncratic statues of *luohans*. Li Guangxiu, a Sichuanese sculptor of wide renown, appalled the conservatives of his time by introducing this traditional Buddhist folk art into temple architecture between 1884 and 1890, while overseeing the restoration of the temple. The painted clay figures were modelled after real personalities and each life-like caricature embodies a Buddhist virtue. Popular belief claims that, by beginning with any statue and counting down the row to your right as far as the number of your age, you will stop at the luohan who best exemplifies your inner self.

The main temple building holds three large Buddha statues— Sakyamuni, the historical Buddha in the middle, the Medicine Buddha on the left, and Amitabha, Lord of the Western Paradise, on the right. Local Buddhists pray and offer incense in front of the three images. Against the hall's left (east) wall stands a stone stele dating from 1314. It is an imperial decree from the Yuan emperor instructing the temple's abbot to collect Buddhist scriptural classics and spread the religion. Written in Mongolian script with a translation into vernacular Chinese, it shows that this must have been a highly influential and politically important temple in the 14th century.

BLACK DRAGON POOL (HEILONGTAN) AND THE BOTANICAL GARDEN (ZHIWUYUAN)

This park and the adjacent botanical garden lie in the Wulao Hills, 17 kilometres (10 miles) northwest of Kunming.

The wooded park with its Black Dragon Pool is the site of a restored Ming-Dynasty temple, once the largest Daoist (Taoist) centre in southwest China. According to legend, the pool contained ten violently destructive dragons. Around the year 750 a reclusive scholar named Lu Dongbin mastered the secrets of Daoism and thereupon set out across China to slay dragons and demons. Reaching this pool, he killed nine of the dragons with his sword but allowed the tenth, a small black one, to remain in the pool on condition that it work for the benefit of mankind. Lu Dongbin is honoured as one of the Daoist Eight Immortals, easily recognized in pictures by his sword and fly-whisk. He is the patron saint of Chinese barbers.

The Daoist temple, perched on a hillside overlooking the pool, is built on three levels. The first contains famous, ancient trees in its courtyards—a Tang-Dynasty plum tree, a Song-Dynasty cypress, a Ming-Dynasty camellia and a Qing-Dynasty magnolia. In front of the temple building is a gigantic bronze *ding,* a tripodal incense burner decorated with the eight trigrams. The second level building now serves as an art gallery for scroll brush paintings. The top level is a restored temple building.

A seven-minute walk from Black Dragon Pool's entrance leads straight to the Kunming Botanical Garden. The entrance to the garden is through a small gate on the left, directly across the road from the imposing entrance to the Botanical Institute. The meticulously kept gardens contain plant specimens from all over Yunnan Province, but are most widely known for the collection of camellias, Yunnan pine (*Pinus yunnunensis*), rhododendrons and azaleas. Greenhouses are at the far end. It is an attractive, well laid-out botanical garden.

COPPER TEMPLE OR GOLDEN TEMPLE (JINDIAN)

This unique Daoist temple lies 11 kilometres (7 miles) northeast of Kunming. By car, it is 10 kilometres (6 miles) from Black Dragon Pool, heading southeast on Longtou Jie. Situated in a pine forest atop Phoenix Song Mountain, the temple requires a climb up a very long flight of stone steps, punctuated by three Heavenly Gates. A fourth gate brings visitors to the entrance of the temple grounds.

Gardens and galleries flank a central path leading to a miniature, medieval city wall complete with a typical gate tower, bell tower and drum tower. Inside, on a terrace of finest Dali marble with elegantly carved railings, stands the little copper temple itself. In Chinese it is still known as the Golden Temple because, when first built, the burnished copper gleamed like gold.

In 1604, the governor of Yunnan and some powerful nobles wished to honour the Daoist hero-god Zishi, who was supposed to live at the northern extremity of the universe. They built the Copper Temple to represent his city-palace there. Three decades later, the temple was transported intact to Jizu Shan (Chicken Foot Mountain), a holy mountain in western Yunnan (see page 106). In 1670, a duplicate temple was cast in deliberate defiance of China's new Manchu emperor, to whom the copper was owed as tribute. This second temple was destroyed in the mid-19th century, during Yunnan's great Muslim rebellion. A new temple was built from parts of the duplicate in 1890. The walls, columns, rafters, roof-tiles, altar, altar-hangings, even the banner near the gate tower, are all made of copper. The whole structure weighs more than 300 tons and stands 6.5 metres (21 feet) high.

Outlying buildings, containing art galleries and a teahouse, are not of great interest. At the summit of the mountain behind the temple, a bizarre, ugly tower, built in 1984, holds a giant bronze bell, so massive that its rim is a full hand span in thickness. Its decorations identify it as a Buddhist relic, not originally a part of this Daoist temple. The huge camellia tree near the temple is 600 years old; in the month of February it produces hundreds of magnificent red blossoms—a sight that should not be missed by late-winter visitors to Kunming.

YUNNAN OBSERVATORY (YUNNAN TIANWENTAI)

An important centre for astronomy is located on Phoenix Hill, 10 kilometres (6 miles) east of Kunming. Over 2,000 metres (6,550 feet) above sea level, the sprawling complex of buildings and silver domes commands an impressive view across the plain and Lake Dianchi to the far distant Western Hill by day, while its telescopes give a clear view of the skies by night.

The Observatory, administered by the Chinese Academy of Sciences, has sections for radio astronomy, solar physics, stellar physics, celestial mechanics and astrometry. A technical laboratory works with new instruments and computers. The one-metre optical telescope—one of the largest in China—is in use approximately 200 nights out of the year. A satellite tracking station and a parabolic radio telescope complete the installation.

The Yunnan Observatory conducts guided tours for the public with lectures, a visit to the small exhibition hall and night-time observation of the moon, planets and stars through a 35-centimetre telescope. Arrangments can be made through CITS or the Observatory.

Yunnan's traditional cooking ware, including the famous copper hot pot

Sights Around Lake Dianchi

Lake Dianchi, 340 square kilometres (132 square miles), is the largest lake in Yunnan and the sixth largest in China. Its length is 40 kilometres (25 miles) and the width at its widest point is 14 kilometres (9 miles).

The lake, capable of tossing up violent storms, is especially beautiful when winds subside and it reflects the ethereal light of dawn or sunset. The Chinese describe the lake's moods as 'virility seasoned with tenderness'. Its shores are dotted with small fishing hamlets surrounded by fertile fields. High rectangular sails ribbed with bamboo battens propel ancient-style wooden boats across the water, though these are fast disappearing. Fishing boats carry a single sail; big three-masted hulls transport rock from lakeside quarries—just as they have done for 2,000 years. In any weather, the mountain-girded lake is a splendid sight and a day trip around its shores is well worth the effort, though in recent years the waters have become polluted and some doctors recommend that people should not swim in the lake.

Interesting places to stop as you follow a clockwise route around Dianchi are listed below. All can be reached by bus. However, for convenience and flexibility while sightseeing, a hired car is recommended.

HAIGENG

This lakeside resort lies 10 kilometres (6 miles) directly south of Kunming. Along the road between Kunming and the lake you will pass through farming villages and pleasant countryside wherever new growth and suburbs have not encroached. Haigeng means 'sea ridge' and lies at the mouth of the Winding Dragon River (Panlong Jiang), the main water course of Kunming.

Haigeng is known as 'Kunming's Riviera' and with an enormous stretch of the imagination you might think it vaguely approaches that. It is extremely popular with local young people during the weekends; here is a roller-skating rink, a small man-made lake with boats for hire, and numerous small shops and restaurants. The main attraction is a long, willow-lined esplanade along the lake front. Two long cement jetties run out into the lake. For the energetic, it is possible to walk from Haigeng to the top of Western Hill, or vice versa. Haigeng has gained some public-ity in China due to an Olympic village and stadium nearby where the nation's top athletes receive training in the high air of Yunnan.

More recently, the lakeside area has tried to attract visitors with the establish-ment of the Haigeng Tourist Centre for Ethnic Cultures. Here, concentrated in one spot, is a reconstruction of the lifestyles and customs of Yunnan's 25 separate minority groups. Some people disdain this kind of 'Ethnic Disneyland', though in fact one can learn quite a lot through a visit. Try to make friends with the people, craftsmen and performers, many who have come from remarkable, distant parts of the mountainous province.

XIAOBANQIAO

This country market town lies 12 kilometres (7.5 miles) southeast of Kunming. Sunday is market day, when peasants, villagers, craftsmen and fishermen from the neighbouring countryside gather for an open-air market, setting up stalls elbow to elbow down the streets and alleys. It is interesting and fun to take part in a genuine, rustic event and you may find something amazing or unique to buy: a pair of flowered peasant shoes, a jade-inlaid pipe, some lovingly crafted hand-tools, a baby pig or an apron embroidered with cranes and camellias.

THE EASTERN SHORE

After Xiaobanqiao, the road leads south for 14 kilometres (9 miles) to the big town of Chenggong, where the road to the Stone Forest branches off to the left. Markets take place in this town, too, but they tend to be more modern and less colourful than the events at Xiaobanqiao. The area south of Chenggong is known for its apple, peach and pear orchards. The succulent pearl pear (*baozhuli*) is a local speciality, much prized for its flavour.

Along the whole stretch of the road heading south, small roads lead enticingly off to the right towards the lake. To follow any one of them is to enter the world of rural Yunnan. You may find a little teahouse, fishermen mending nets, an ancient, forgotten pagoda or a tiny harbour with a boat landing its catch.

The old county town of Jincheng, 14 kilometres (9 miles) beyond Chenggong, is a good place to stop for a cup of tea. Five kilometres west of it is the archaeological site of Shizhaishan, a hill where 48 Bronze Age tombs yielded a trove of art treasures in 1955.

Passing around the southern end of the lake, the next sizeable town is Jinning, formally called Kunyang, birthplace of the great 15th-century explorer Zheng He. The white skull-caps of the Muslims, the black turbans of the Han, the fur-fringed hats of the Yi, all reflect the ethnic mixture in this area. Zheng He, the Eunuch Admiral, was himself a Muslim. He is the town's most revered native son. Each year, his descendants gather here from all parts of China to celebrate the Muslim festival of Qurban Bayran. See Special Topic 'The Eunuch Admiral', page 182.

A museum honouring Zheng He, his family and his accomplishments stands north of Jinning at Yueshan (Moon Hill), which is also known as Zheng He Park. It

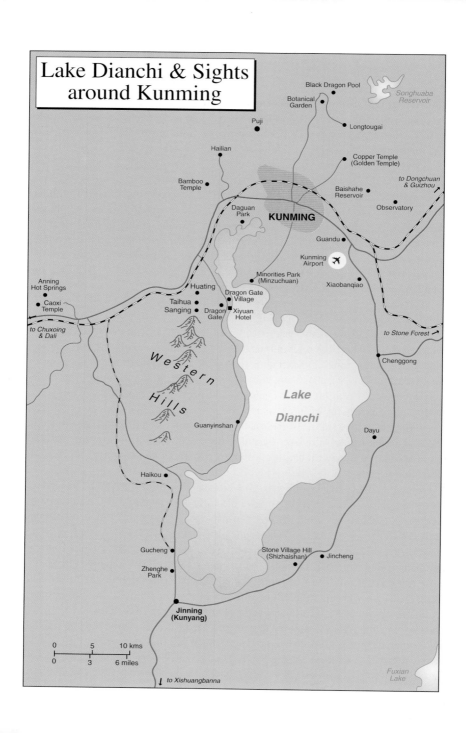

Lake Dianchi & Sights around Kunming

Black Dragon Pool

Songhuaba Reservoir

Botanical Garden

Puji

Longtougai

Hailian

Copper Temple (Golden Temple)

Bamboo Temple

to Dongchuan & Guizhou

Baishahe Reservoir

Daguan Park

KUNMING

Observatory

Guandu

Kunming Airport

Minorities Park (Minzuchuan)

Xiaobanqiao

Anning Hot Springs

Huating

Caoxi Temple

Taihua Sanging

Dragon Gate Village

Dragon Gate

Xiyuan Hotel

to Chuxoing & Dali

to Stone Forest

Chenggong

W e s t e r n

H i l l s

Lake Dianchi

Guanyinshan

Dayu

Haikou

Gucheng

Stone Village Hill (Shizhaishan)

Jincheng

Zhenghe Park

Jinning (Kunyang)

0	5	10 kms
0	3	6 miles

to Xishuangbanna

Fuxian Lake

is a well-kept, impressive museum for such a small town and worth a stop. Even the buildings on the hill have been built to resemble ocean-going junks.

ZHENG HE PARK AND MUSEUM (ZHENG HE GONGYUAN)

The focus of this sprawling, somewhat run-down park is the museum itself, housed in an elaborately reconstructed Buddhist temple. The only sight worth mentioning in the park is the tomb of Zheng He's father, the haji, which lies near the walkway. The original 600-year-old stele tells the family's history and exploits in Chinese characters that are still legible.

The museum's first room contains rubbings from many different steles telling of Zheng He's deeds. The most important is from the 1,170-character stele, the Zheng He Inscription Stone, which stands in the coastal city of Quanzhou in Fujian Province, chronicling his seven great voyages. The second room holds examples of the Chinese products which Zheng He took in his ships to trade abroad, notably Ming pottery known as Dragon Spring (longquan) ware. Examples have been found in Java, Sri Lanka, Africa and many other points along his routes. This room also displays photographs of these and other sites where his ships touched shore, as well as some indifferent modern paintings recreating scenes from Zheng He's diplomatic encounters.

Upstairs there are fine, clear diagrams and charts of Zheng He's huge ships, some capable of carrying over 500 men. The dimensions of their towering masts are shown, along with the anchors and sails. Navigational instruments include a complicated compass. The walls are covered with good maps that show in detail the extent of his trips and landfalls.

HAIKOU AND BAIYUKOU

Heading north along the western shore of Lake Dianchi, the first big town is Haikou, several kilometres inland. It is an unprepossessing, industrial town redeemed by the numerous restaurants along the main road which offer good, simple fare. At Haikou, the Praying Mantis River (Tanglang Chuan) carries the waters of Lake Dianchi to the Yangzi River at the border of Sichuan Province, then on to the East China Sea.

Baiyukou, a resort centred on a big sanatorium, lies on the lake 10 kilometres (6 miles) north of Haikou. The spacious health centre, set aside for Kunming's workers, has attractive gardens and grounds running down to the water's edge; these are open to the public. A handsome stone mansion, the country retreat of a pre-revolutionary mayor of Kunming, has been appropriated by the sanitorium. Causeways lined by willow trees, symbols of spring and friendship, enclose miniature lakes. There are pleasant walks among pine and eucalyptus woods behind Baiyukou, and caves to explore.

A ferry boat makes a round trip from Kunming to Baiyukou once a day. If you are not in a hurry, the water route is a picturesque and leisurely way to make the trip, either coming or going.

GUANYINSHAN TEMPLE (GUANYINSHAN SI)

From Baiyukou, looking north along the shore, you can see a ruined pagoda on a promontory named Guanyin Shan. On the hillside behind the pagoda stands a charming little Ming-Dynasty temple, hidden in the woods. A steep, unpaved track runs up to it from the left side of the main road. A few monks and nuns take care of the Buddhist shrine, which is dedicated to Guanyin, the Goddess of Mercy. They welcome visitors to the main temple building, the most ancient in the small complex. Its worn stone floor, banners of orange, red, pink and yellow silk, the burning candles and incense all imbue the small temple with warmth and intimacy. Peasants are likely to drop in, to place offerings of tangerines and wine before the Buddha statues and especially before the goddess herself.

A brief walk down to the ruined pagoda, Guanyin Ta, gives a magnificent view of red mountains, blue water and innumerable shades of green in the fields below. The highly visible pagoda was built centuries ago at this spot to be seen from all directions as a beacon to the Buddhist faithful. It was ruined, like many Buddhist monuments, during the Muslim rebellion in the mid-19th century.

The main road north goes for 18 kilometres (11 miles) from Guanyin Shan to the bus stop at the base of Western Hill and then on to Kunming.

ANNING HOT SPRINGS (ANNING WENQUAN)

The bustling eounty seat of Anning lies 34 kilometres (21 miles) southwest of Kunming on the famous old Burma Road that now serves as the main east-west highway of Yunnan. The hot springs are at the centre of a spa 8 kilometres (5 miles) north of Anning.

The springs were discovered two thousand years ago in the Han Dynasty and Anning has been a favourite bathing spot ever since. Foreigners may find it a far cry from Baden Baden, but the happy grins of parboiled Chinese will attest to its continuing popularity. The odourless mineral water bubbles up at an average temperature of 42° C (102° F). In fact, virtually all hot springs in China are far less enticing compared to their counterparts in Japan, Europe or North America.

CAOXI TEMPLE AND FAHUA TEMPLE GROTTOES

A trip to Anning should absolutely include visits to two nearby Buddhist sites: Caoxi Temple and the Fahua Temple Grottoes.

Caoxi Temple is 2 kilometres south of the hot springs. It is the only remaining Song-Dynasty (960–1279) structure in the Kunming area. Legend says that a monk in the year 502 was so beguiled by the quality of the local water that he founded a temple here. The temple's subsequent history included patronage by Huineng, one of Chan (Zen) Buddhism's greatest patriarchs. Among the precious, wooden, Song-Dynasty sculptures, the central Buddha is noted for a remarkable event that takes place once every 60 years. The September full moon that marks China's Mid-Autumn Festival then shines through a small hole in the temple's roof, placing a medallion of silvery moonlight on the Buddha's forehead.

The Fahua Temple Grottoes are all that remain of a Song-Dynasty Buddhist temple in the cliffs behind Xiao Taohua Cun, a village 5 kilometres (3 miles) east of the town of Anning. The hill itself is known as Luoyang Shan, and the carvings date from the late 13th or early 14th century. Eighteen luohans are carved in three vertical rows of different sizes on the cliff's east side, and near these holy men are scenes from the Jattaka, instructive tales from the Buddha's former lives. To the south of the cliff lies a large reclining Buddha, 4.2 metres (14 feet) long. This is the historical Buddha Sakyamuni at his moment of death and entry into nirvana; this scene, in stone and in paintings, is known as the Buddha's *Parinirvana*. Nearby are statues of Guanyin and Dizang (Sanskrit: *Kshitigarbha*), the latter a bodhisattva venerated in folk belief as a saviour from the torments of Hell and helper of deceased children. Sometimes he is also regarded as a protector of travellers.

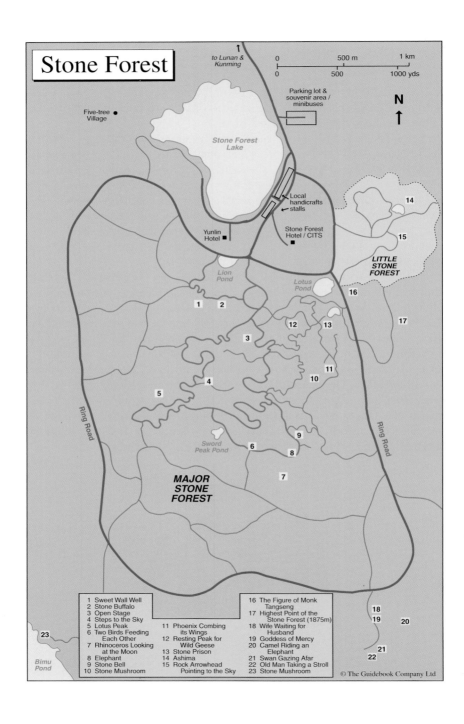

Stone Forest

to Lunan & Kunming

| 0 | | 500 m | | 1 km |
| 0 | | 500 | | 1000 yds |

Parking lot & souvenir area / minibuses

N

Five-tree Village

Stone Forest Lake

Local handicrafts stalls

Yunlin Hotel

Stone Forest Hotel / CITS

LITTLE STONE FOREST

Lion Pond

Lotus Pond

1   2

12   13   14

3   15

16

17

5

4   10   11

Ring Road

9

Sword Peak Pond

6   8

7

MAJOR STONE FOREST

Ring Road

18
19   20

21
22

23

Bimu Pond

1 Sweet Wall Well
2 Stone Buffalo
3 Open Stage
4 Steps to the Sky
5 Lotus Peak
6 Two Birds Feeding
   Each Other
7 Rhinoceros Looking
   at the Moon
8 Elephant
9 Stone Bell
10 Stone Mushroom

11 Phoenix Combing
   its Wings
12 Resting Peak for
   Wild Geese
13 Stone Prison
14 Ashima
15 Rock Arrowhead
   Pointing to the Sky

16 The Figure of Monk
   Tangseng
17 Highest Point of the
   Stone Forest (1875m)
18 Wife Waiting for
   Husband
19 Goddess of Mercy
20 Camel Riding an
   Elephant
21 Swan Gazing Afar
22 Old Man Taking a Stroll
23 Stone Mushroom

© The Guidebook Company Ltd

The Stone Forest (Shilin)

The Stone Forest is the name given to an extremely rare geological phenomenon 126 kilometres (79 miles) southeast of Kunming. It is not a 'Petrified Forest' (like the one found in Arizona) but 80 hectares (200 acres) of karst limestone pillars in fantastic shapes that, from a distance, resemble a forest.

About 270 million years ago, during the Permian Period, this area was covered by water. Later, due to shifts in the earth's crust, the ocean slowly receded while the limestone sea bed rose up to form a tableland. Rain and seeping water ate away at the limestone surface. The stone eroded in different places, causing fissures to open around small pinnacles. In time, acidic rain devoured most of the limestone, leaving the huge, isolated, but densely packed stone pillars that can be seen today in the middle of Lunan County. The Stone Forest, one of the main attractions of Yunnan, is the home of the Sani people, who make up a branch of the diverse and scattered Yi tribe.

Getting to the Stone Forest

There are several ways to reach the Stone Forest. Tourist groups travel there by private bus, but there are also numerous public buses and vans bound for the Stone Forest every day. A private car, though more expensive, can get to the Stone Forest in less than two hours.

The least used but most interesting way to get to the Stone Forest is to use a combination of train and bus. Early this century, the French built a narrow-guage railway to link their colonial capital of Hanoi, in Indochina, with Kunming. The line, which opened in 1910, snakes across craggy mountains and lush valleys on its way southeast to the Vietnamese border. Tourists can take this charming little train to the county seat of Yiliang, two-thirds of the way to the Stone Forest, and travel the remaining 36 kilometres (22.5 miles) by bus. Yiliang's bus station is on the left side of the main road just before the chief intersection as you walk into town. The train leaves from Kunming's North Station (Bei Zhan) every morning and chugs along at barely 40 kilometres (25 miles) per hour, allowing you to see Yunnan's pleasant countryside. Small stations are built in French style, with painted shutters and steep roofs. After crossing a high, barren mountain pass, the train makes a big curve to the left. Far below, on the right, is Yangzong Hai, a wild, blue lake about 15 kilometres (9 miles) from Yiliang. A strong walker might want to alight at

Karst limestone pillars of the Stone Forest

Yangzong Hai Station, walk down the sparsely inhabited mountain to the lake shore, have a picnic, then walk on to the county seat.

Yiliang is a medium-sized town at the centre of a rich agricultural area, small enough to explore in a couple of hours. The market along its main street is a full-blown country event. The citadel at the centre of the old town gives a fine view over curly-eaved roofs, temples and lanes. A new railway line connecting Kunming with Guangxi to the east will one day link the capital directly with the Stone Forest.

Sights at the Stone Forest

As should be expected with such a unique natural area, legends abound in Sani folklore about the Stone Forest. Its creation legend is a Promethean fable.

A Sani youth named Jinfeng Roga was ambitious and bold, but also caring. He wanted to save the local farmers from drought by building a great dam to catch the waters. One night he sneaked into the crypt of the gods and stole their talisman, a magic whip capable of moving mountains. All through the night, the hero drove rocky hills like a flock of sheep towards the town of Yiliang, his chosen dam site. But the crowing cocks signalled daybreak before his task was finished, and the talisman lost its power. The hills stopped fast and became the Stone Forest. Jinfeng Roga was soon captured and brutally murdered by the gods. His martyrdom is recalled by long cracks in the rocks, said to be the whip weals inflicted on his body.

Another more romantic legend is told throughout Yunnan in song, story and dance-drama. It concerns a beautiful Sani girl named Ashima and her brother Ahei. Ashima and her family lived happily among their tribe until a wicked magician carried her off to his castle. After many trials and tribulations, Ahei rescued his sister. With freedom almost in their grasp, the siblings fled through the 12 mighty crags of the Stone Forest. Here a flood, unleashed by the magician, swept Ashima away, separating her forever from her brother and the idyllic life of her people. Ashima's aura appeared above the Stone Forest and her spirit lived on there as an echo. Ashima has been immortalized in the natural formation of a limestone rock, one which resembles a young girl, within the Little Stone Forest.

The Chinese delight in projecting their imagination onto nature (*ad nauseam*). Almost every prominent peak in the rock jungle bears a name, such as Mother and Son Going for a Walk, Rhinoceros Looking at the Moon, Phoenix Preening its Wings, or A Camel Riding an Elephant.

A gravel road about 7 kilometres (4.5 miles) long encircles the whole area. It can take you away from crowded tourist areas into open countryside with the Stone

Forest forming a backdrop. On the northern stretch there is a sizeable lake and, nearby, Wushu Cun (Five Tree Village), a typical Sani settlement well known for its craftsmen and musicians. Outside the southern limit of the circular road are several clusters of natural stone sculptures. Paths lead southward towards rarely visited traditional Sani villages. If you leave the gravel road, you might consider taking a stick to ward off unfriendly dogs.

The colourful Sani people around the Stone Forest are highly attuned to tourists. Their handicrafts, especially bags and clothing with beautiful embroidery and appliqué work, are on sale in profusion. Performances of rousing Sani dances, music and songs are held each evening.

The highlight of each year at the Stone Forest is the Torch Festival, which takes place on June 24th of the lunar calendar (late July or early August). It is a gala of horse-racing, bullfighting, wrestling, music, drinking and dancing, drawing together Sani people from all over Lunan County. The climax at nightfall is a torch-light parade through the Stone Forest accompanied by elephant drums, flutes and Sani lutes.

The town of Lunan lies 7 kilometres (4.5 miles) southwest of the Stone Forest. It can be reached by heading back along the Kunming road for 4 kilometres (2.5 miles), then taking the only paved road to the left. The market buzzes with activity, and this is the departure point for a 35-kilometre (21-mile) trip to Dadishui, Yunnan's largest waterfall.

ALU GROTTOES (ALU GUDONG)

A further 80 kilometres (50 miles) east of the Stone Forest is Yunnan's most recent tourist attraction, a series of huge subterranean grottoes with nearly three kilometres of pathways. Here underground rivers, illuminated stalagmites, 'stone flowers' and karst formations of every description await the eager visitor. People interested in caves will enjoy Alu; they can even stay at a local hotel and eat buckwheat products of the local Yi minority.

QUJING

Qujing is a small city on the main rail line 155 kilometres northeast of Kunming, half way between Yunnan's capital and the Guizhou border. It makes a convenient stop for travellers on their way to Guiyang or Guilin, or for those who want to see an unspoilt market town where few foreigners venture. Minority people in the area include Hui, Miao, Yi and others.

The city, on a broad plain (altitude: 1880 metres), has been a historical crossroad. More than two thousand years ago it was an important stop on the imperial Post Route and for centuries Qujing was a key station along the Southwest Silk Route that transported goods, people and ideas to Burma, India and beyond.

Forty seven kilometres north of Qujing is the source of the West River (Xi Jiang), China's third most important after the Yellow and Yangzi rivers. The point of origin is the eastern face of the Maxiong Mountains (Maxiong Shan); a small resort for holidaymakers stands near here.

Also north of the city, some 30 kilometres away between Yanfang and Songlin, is a section of ancient road, known as the Five-*chi* Post Route. The name refers to the width of the trail; one *chi* is slightly more than one foot. This is one of China's oldest surviving roads.

Torch Festival of the Sani People, The Stone Forest

Central Yunnan

The Lake Region

Kunming, Lake Dianchi and the watered regions to the south can be considered Yunnan's heartland. They saw the development more than three thousand years ago of a unique Bronze-Age culture (see pages 44–46), and through the centuries have been vital to the agriculture, transportation and politics of the province. The counties that follow the lakes southward have prospered since the Yuan and Ming dynasties and make up the most populous parts of Yunnan.

Lakes are a major characteristic of Central Yunnan's topography. A look at the provincial map reveals a string of lakes that commences in Kunming's southern suburbs and extends southward for 150 kilometers (95 miles), halfway to the Vietnamese border. The lakes are: Dianchi, Yangzong Hai, Fuxian Hu, Xingyun Hu, Qili Hu and Yilong Hu. A brief description of the lakes follows.

LAKE DIANCHI

At an altitude of 1886 metres, with a surface area of 300 square kilometres, Dianchi is Yunnan's largest lake, though it is only 8 metres (28 feet) at its deepest point. For an account this important lake and a sightseeing trip around it, see pages 58–63.

YANGZONG HAI

This deep, blue body of water is seldom visited. It lies near the rail line and falls mostly within Yiliang County, directly east of Lake Dianchi. A tiny station on the narrow guage rail allows one the chance to get off and explore the grassy, treeless shores of Yangzong Hai. The word *hai* in the lake's name means 'sea'; because of Yunnan's remoteness from the actual ocean, large bodies of water are sometimes called *hai*, not *hu*, the more common name for a lake.

FUXIAN HU

The name of the lake means 'nurture the immortals'. It is Yunnan's third largest lake (after Dianchi and Erhai) at 212 square kilometres and China's second deepest (after Tianchi in Jilin Province) at 151.5 metres (500 feet). Fuxian Hu is wide and deep in the north and contains one island in the southwest. The western edge has steep mountains coming right down to the shore, but elsewhere there are villages and fine agricultural fields, and here and there bubble hot springs. Fishing in the clear water usually takes place at night or along the shores in special 'trapping channels' called *yugou*, or 'fish-ditches'.

A short river called Haimen (*'sea gate'*) connects Fuxian Hu with its neighbour to the west, Xingyun Hu. Here stands a curious three-character stele in the hand of Emperor Qianlong (1736–95), the Fish Border Stele. It marks the extent of where fish from each lake are willing to roam before returning to their own waters. Fish from one lake never pass into the other.

XINGYUN HU

This lake, at 1722 metres, lies one metre higher than Fuxian Hu. It is only 40 square kilometres in extent and 10 metres (33 feet) deep. Its name means 'lake of stars and clouds', a reference to the water's reflections on nights of silvery moonlight. Haixi hot springs, a small resort, are on the lake's west side.

QILI HU

This lake, sometimes known as Tonghai, lies just north of the county town of that name. Overlooking the waters is Xiu Shan, one of Yunnan's important Buddhist sites, a mountain formerly covered with temples and monasteries.

YILONG HU

The lake's name in Chinese means 'strange dragon', though the etymology goes back to the Yi language, from which the sounds *yiluo* ('water city') were borrowed and adapted. The original, indigenous name refers to two of the lake's three islands, Water City Isle and Lesser Water City Isle, though the link with the Chinese appellation might be a reference to underwater palaces of the dragon-kings. A third island, called Mabaolong, was said to be infested by snakes and only fit for outlaws and bandits. Yilong Hu sits at 1414 metres and is the province's fourth largest lake.

Towns of Central Yunnan

CHENGGONG

This town on the east shore of Lake Dianchi has been an important market centre for over 700 years. A Yuan-Dynasty chronicle mentions 'markets crowded with Han and tribal peoples; shells are used as currency'. The main market, known as *laogai* ('old market' or 'old street') still flourishes, as do colourful, rustic tea houses.

CHENGJIANG

Chengjiang is another market town and county centre just north of Fuxian Hu. The town retains some excellent wooden architecture. At the base of Liangwang Shan, a 2825-metre mountain, lies a pond known as Xilong Chi, and around it are temples and buildings from the Ming and Qing dynasties. Longquan Si (Dragon Spring Temple) has an outstanding altar with marble legs of fantastic, mythic animals, more reminiscent of Hindu creatures than Chinese Buddhist beasts. The temple stands four kilometres northwest of Chengjiang.

YUXI

This large town southwest of Chengjiang is known as 'Tobacco City', the major processing centre for Yunnan's renowned cigarettes.

In the suburbs is the village of Wayao Cun, where excavations have revealed porcelain kilns. These confirm that during the Yuan Dynasty, when many soldiers and refugees settled here from eastern China, some came from Jingdezhen, the famous pottery centre in Jiangxi Province. In time, competition from outside closed down the inferior kilns of Central Yunnan.

JIANGCHUAN

The town's name means 'rivers and plains', a good description of the surrounding fertile basin. Jiangchuan county is the home of Shizhai Shan, one of the important Bronze-Age sites of Central Yunnan; humans have thrived here for millennia. Majestic Qing-Dynasty gate towers still stand in Jiangchuan's old section.

TONGHAI

In the early 14th century, troops from seven provinces were brought here to protect the strategic route southward and the border of the empire. The real limit of Yuan power in the southwest ended here. In 1381, with the fall of the Yuan in Yunnan, the Mongol garrison stationed at Tonghai was unable to go home. As Yunnan was the last area to hold out against the Ming, this internal exile was a kind of punishment.

Eight kilometres (five miles) west of Tonghai is Xinmeng (New Mongolia), a remarkable community of three clustered villages that is home to Yunnan's 6000 Mongolians, stranded remnants of the long-lost army. In time 'the horsemen' became known as 'the fishermen', though today Tonghai's Mongols are famous as carpenters and bricklayers. They even consider Lu Ban, China's patron saint of builders, to be a Mongol. A local Guanyin temple has, side-by-side, the Goddess of Mercy, Genghis Khan and Lu Ban!

The transition from soldiers and horsemen to farmers and fishermen was helped

A Tale of Yunnan

When heaven and earth were first clearly divided, the world was not so bright as it is today. It was only a vast expanse of murky grey. The sun, moon, and stars did not exist. At that time a poor woman and her three daughters lived together in the woods. The three sisters were named Hosuni, Dosuni, and Bisuni.

One day, the mother was getting ready to go out, and before she left the house, she warned her girls, "I'm going to look for something for us to eat. Keep the door locked, and stay home. Don't go out and don't open the door. I'll be back before long." And off she went.

The three daughters waited and waited inside the house for their mother to come back, but a long, long time passed, and still she had not returned.

In the forest there was a leopard-demon who had ever been scheming how to allure the daughters to leave their house so he could eat them, but he could never find a way, simply because Hosuni, Dosuni, and Bisuni were so closely guarded by their mother. That particular day, he realized the mother had been gone an awfully long while, so he passed by their door, disguised as a young man singing a folk song. At first, the three sisters were astonished to hear someone sing, and then they were scared. But the more they listened to the song, the more they liked what they heard. Surely it was a young man, after all! Convinced the leopard-demon really was a youth singing folk songs, the three girls opened the door and walked in the direction of his voice. But once they got near and had a look, they realized that their young man was none other than a leopard-demon in disguise. Then and there, they changed direction, and ran for home. Wearing a big grin on his face, the leopard-demon gave chase, intending to catch the three sisters, but they quickly scurried up a tree. The leopard-demon tried to climb up too, but he couldn't do it.

"Hey, girls!" he said, unctuously. "I'm here on a visit to see my relatives. Rest assured I wouldn't do you any harm. Won't you please just teach me how to climb a tree? If you do, I will remember your kindness my whole, entire life long."

Hosuni and Dosuni refused to trust the leopard-demon, and wouldn't tell him a thing. But their littlest sister, Bisuni, didn't know any better, and she blurted *out, unthinkingly, "Why, there's nothing at all to tree climbing! All you have to do is start with your hands, and then use your feet, back and forth, back and forth." It was much too late now for the two older sisters to shush up Bisuni. The leopard-demon climbed the tree, following the little girl's advice, alternating his front paws and back legs.*

Ever since that day, leopards have known how to climb trees.

When Hosuni, Dosuni, and Bisuni saw that the leopard-demon had learned to climb, they were so nervous that they headed straight for the top of the tree. But the leopard-demon followed right behind. At that point, the three girls all bawled at the top of their lungs in a fit of despair.

Now it just so happened that a god from heaven was passing by. He was enormously sympathetic. "Little girls, now stop crying. I can save you by taking you to heaven. But there is just one problem: once you are up there, you can't come back down here. How would you feel about that?" Seeing the leopard-demon was getting closer and closer, Hosuni, Dosuni, and Bisuni hastily agreed that they liked the idea very much. Raising his hand on high, the god took them up to heaven.

After they got to heaven, the three lived quite happily, but they missed their dear mother, and they longed to see the good earth again. So they earnestly pleaded with the god to let them return. The god said, "You may take turns. Since Hosuni is the eldest, let her go first. After that, Dosuni, then Bisuni." So, Hosuni went first. After she came back, Dosuni and Bisuni had a turn. Each of them got to visit their mother, and see the earth, the forest, and the river where they had once lived.

When their mother had returned home, and found that her daughters were missing, she had looked for them everywhere, but could not find them. She got to see them, however, when they came visiting. But now they were in heaven, while she was on earth, and no longer could they live together.

Every day, Hosuni and her sisters would take turns seeing their mother and the earth. In the course of time, Hosuni became the sun, while Dosuni and Bisuni became the moon and the stars. From then on, there was day and night. Sometimes, Dosuni and Bisuni appear together, and at other times, the younger sister comes out all by herself. That's why, at night, sometimes the moon and the stars appear at the same time, and at other times only the stars can be seen.

From *South of the Clouds*, edited by Lucien Miller, 1994

by supernatural intervention. A holy vision of a man on a rhinoceros came to the Mongols; the beast led them out to the lake to reveal a golden temple and an image of 'a fish carrying food'. They followed the vision and forever more became known as 'the fishermen'.

It is said that the Mongolian spoken here has retained many archaisms and cannot be understood by Mongolians from the north. Traditional heavy robes were changed to cotton because of the warm land, were shortened because of the demands of fishing and sleeves were abandoned when they became carpenters and builders. The result of these changes is a kind of short robe, very attractive and colourful, resembling a jacket. Hairstyles for women changed from a large bun to a sweet, simpler form with two tails sticking out, like cowlicks.

Muslims and Mongols make up a considerable part of the region's population. A mosque at Gucheng Village displays a mixture of Chinese and Persian features. Xiaoxin Village, near Gucheng, holds the Three Sage Temple whose side gate is surmounted by a weird, elaborate carving of a mythical beast that drinks through a straw the contents of a vessel held by a miniature man riding a white ox.

In Hexi Zhen is the Yuanming Temple, a magnificent late-Yuan complex built between 1341–68. Remaining today is a robust, heavy marble altar with ten carved relief panels and beasts as legs. The carvings show agricultural scenes and a lively, stylized geography. The temple still has exquisite wood carvings and the Pavilion of the Jade Emperor is guarded by two worthy stone lions.

SHIPING

Far to the south of Tonghai, just above Yilong Hu, is the large town of Shiping, a former centre of the Flower-Belt Yi but now mostly inhabited by Han Chinese. The Yi tend to live in villages and suburbs.

Between 1368–98, General Mu Ying of the Ming and his troops 'opened up this wasteland'. Many of the settlers came from Jiangsu and Zhejiang Provinces, and they took their tradition of Confucian studies seriously. They built a Confucian Temple in Shiping, established academies and sent many of their sons to the Imperial Examinations.

JIANSHUI

East of Shiping and Yilong Hu is Jianshui, formerly called Lin'an, an alternative name for the great city of Hangzhou in Zhejiang Province. So Jianshui became Hangzhou West, or so it was conceived by the Ming troops and immigrants who settled in Central Yunnan in their tens of thousands. Many artisans and their families did indeed come from Hangzhou.

Parts of the old city wall still stand, faded by time to a soft russet red, though unquestionably Jianshui's greatest site is its Confucian Temple. Begun in 1325 and recipient of over 50 renovations, it is China's second largest Confucian temple, after the one in Qufu, Confucius's home town. The temple complex runs along a 625-metre-long axis and comprises six courtyards and 114 buildings. The main temple is in the fifth courtyard. Fine carvings, woodwork, plaques and architecture try to immitate the grandeur of the mother-temple in Shandong Province. At the complex's entrance is Xuehai Pond where an inscription reads: 'All officials, soldiers, or common people must dismount here!'

The Confucian Temple became the focus of scholarship and the hopes of exiles. The system of Imperial Examinations was the only way up and out of Jianshui, though in time the immigrants came to call their adopted home not only 'Hangzhou' but 'Shandong in southern Yunnan'. They founded academies, rebuilt their lives and supported the temple as an impetus for education in the entire area.

The ancient East Gate of the city still stands and here and there, still in use, are stone-lined wells sunk nearly six centuries ago. At the edge of town is the Seventeen-Arch Bridge, a Qing-Dynasty masterpiece built of stone. It is one of the best examples of its type in all China. Jianshui's most famous product is the ceramic Yunnan steam pot (*qiguo*). See Food and Drink, pages 19–21.

Forty kilometres southeast of Jianshui is the village of Heixin Cun. Here is the old *yamen* (government office), known as the Nalou Headman's Office. During the Ming Dynasty, loyal tribal leaders were put in charge of non-Han areas, and this outpost was handled by a Yi chief. The present complex, with a fine entranceway and huge, upturned eaves, was built in the early 20th century. Four bastions stand at the four corners and the basic, solid Yi style is relieved by Chinese tiles, eaves and gateways.

GEJIU

Gejiu is a large industrial city of southern Yunnan, on a branch rail line southeast of Jianshui. Tin is the reason for Gejiu's existence.

Han Chinese dominate the city and the mines, though all around are people of the Yi, Hani, Miao and Yao minority groups. The city has parks and the Yunmiao Temple.

Boat and stone village, Erhai Lake

Dali

Dali is the capital of the Dali Bai Autonomous Prefecture west of Kunming, a large region made up of 12 counties. It is the historic home of the Bai minority, one of Yunnan's most numerous and prosperous ethnic groups. The name Dali refers to several things: Dali City (Dali Shi), the administrative centre that includes Xiaguan, the main metropolis and Yunnan's second largest city; the old stone town, known formally as Dali Old City (Dali Gu Cheng); and the general surrounding region of towns, villages and Erhai Lake. The old town of weathered gray granite stands at 1,900 metres (6,232 feet) on a long, narrow rice plain between the Azure Mountains (Cangshan) and the bright blue Ear Lake (Erhai), a natural configuration that seems specially designed for a good, bountiful life. In late winter, when fields of brilliant yellow rapeseed shimmer and sway between snow-capped mountains and the sapphire lake, one can agree with the Bai that theirs is the most blessed spot on earth.

The lake, named for its ear-like shape, lies in a geological fault between parallel mountain ranges, south of the great river trenches of eastern Tibet. Erhai Lake, 41 kilometres (30 miles) long and 3 to 9 kilometres (2 to 5 miles) wide, is part of the Mekong River system. The small Xi'er River, fed by glaciers and snow water, enters the lake at its northern end through Dragon's Head Pass. It leaves the lake's southwest corner by a canal at Xiaguan, but soon tumbles boisterously through the Cangshan at Dragon's Tail Pass, a cleft so narrow that a boulder stuck between cliffs forms a natural bridge above it.

The Cangshan range stands like a wall behind Dali's plain, with a long, looping skyline shaped by 19 peaks averaging about 4,000 metres (13,000 feet). Unlike the craggy ranges piled up elsewhere in western Yunnan, the Cangshan alone is made of granite, thrusting up through the earth's limestone crust. Its rich deposits of high quality marble add to Dali's prosperity, and it provides the deep, black earth of the plain at its foot, a contrast to Yunnan's typical red clay.

The plain, 56 kilometres (35 miles) long but only three or four kilometres (two or three miles) wide, is watered by 18 perennial mountain streams, which farmers channel to every plot and terrace. The 19 peaks and 18 streams are the emblems of Dali. Towns and villages perch on the mountain's lower slopes or on the lake shore, keeping the entire plain for agriculture. Rice grows abundantly in summer and autumn; beans and wheat are secondary crops. In former times, Dali thrived on its winter opium crops, until the Chinese government suppressed the trade in the 1930s.

The eastern shore of Erhai Lake is totally different. The low, barren, Red Rocky Mountains (Hongshi Shan) rise directly from the water, with small villages clinging to the foothills. Although receiving little rain, the sparse, red soil is good for peach and pear orchards. Fishing is the main occupation of this shore, for Erhai Lake contains more than 40 varieties of fish. Bai boat owners also transport building materials around the lake, and nowadays match the Bai farmers in prosperity.

Bai means 'white' but the origin of this name is not clear. It has nothing to do with skin colour or colour of dress—Bai women wear a variety of brightly coloured costumes. They call themselves Speakers of the White Language, a tongue distinct from Mandarin, or People of the White King, though the king's identity is lost in conflicting myths.

Dali, their ancestral home, is a town of some 15,000 inhabitants. It lies three kilometres (two miles) from the lake shore, under the highest peak of the Cangshan, roughly in the middle of the plain. The city of Xiaguan, 15 kilometres (nine miles) south, occupies the southwest corner of the lake. Xiaguan began as a trade centre at the crossing of two major caravan routes, linking China with Burma, and eastern Tibet with the tea plantations of southern Yunnan. Xiaguan remains the more important commercial centre, whereas Dali has historically been a seat of cultural and political power.

Dali was the capital of an independent kingdom named Nanzhao during the eighth and ninth centuries, while the Tang Dynasty reigned in China. At its height, Nanzhao conquered much of Burma, attacked parts of Laos and Thailand, and repeatedly invaded China's Sichuan region in a border war that helped to weaken the Tang Dynasty. The royal family of Nanzhao came to an end in 902, when the Chief Minister murdered the infant heir to the throne and proceeded to wipe out all other members of the family as well, initiating decades of turmoil. In 937, a Bai official usurped the throne and renamed the realm the Kingdom of Dali. It prospered for three more centuries, until Kublai Khan conquered it in the autumn of 1253 and made it an outpost of China.

Under the Song Dynasty (960–1279), China's army faced a grave crisis when it lost its steady supply of horses. Wars in the north deprived it of vast pastures and traditional horse-breeding grounds. The Kingdom of Dali provided the solution. Yunnan's breed of strong horses had been known for centuries to the Chinese, who prized the animals for their endurance. About the year 1130, Dali began delivering 1,500 horses a year to the Song government, in exchange for silk, silver and salt.

Fine horses are still traded in Dali. For over a thousand years, the Bai have staged a great annual fair on the open land outside Dali's west gate. The Third Month Fair (Sanyue Jie) of the lunar calendar takes place each year in April. This fair evolved from religious gatherings in which Buddhist monks, disciples and laymen met on the Dali Plain at the time of the third full moon to pray, fast, chant and preach. Fruits and flowers, incense and oil were the main devotional offerings

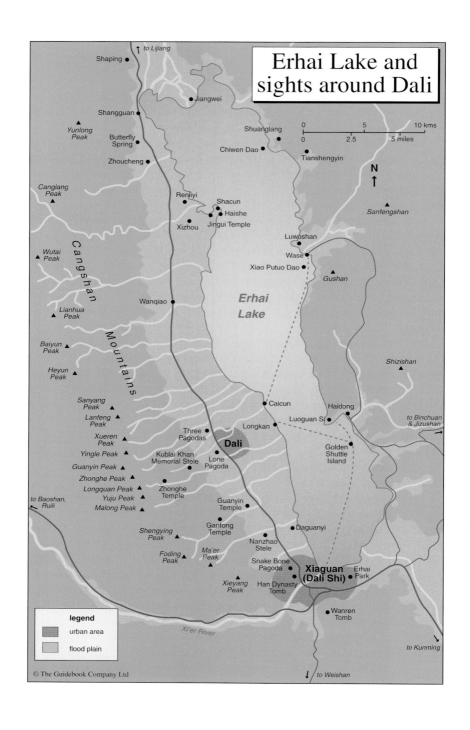

and in time, with the growth of the annual worship festival and subsequent social interchange, trade naturally followed to fulfill the material needs of the faithful. Today, mountain tribes and buyers from many parts of China gather for five days of trading, horse-racing and traditional games. A city of tents and booths springs up, livestock of every sort can be found mooing, bleating and squealing in the animal market, but the fair's greatest drawing power nowadays comes from the rare herbs and medicines that Tibetans and others bring down from the remote mountains on Yunnan's borders. Ranking second to medicines are horses, ridden bareback or in full regalia around a small racetrack to show off their speed and prowess.

With all Dali's prosperity, its famous marble and rich agriculture, with its colourful and vigorous life, it is small wonder that the Bai people consider Dali the best spot in China and never want to leave it.

Getting to Dali

The largest city in the Dali region is Xiaguan at the southwest end of Erhai Lake, 15 kilometres (9 miles) south of Dali. All transport goes to Xiaguan first.

The Dali-Erhai Lake region lies exactly 400 kilometres (250 miles) west of Kunming; this route is part of the famous Burma Road, which acted as Free China's lifeline to the outside world during the early part of World War II. Today it remains the main east-west highway in Yunnan. The trip takes seven or eight hours by car, and a few hours longer by bus. Though this may seem long and rigorous, it is an exciting experience to roll through hills and mountains, occasionally coming out onto broad plains, sharing the road with trucks, jeeps, wheelbarrows, oxen and horse carts. The bus stops two or three times en route at food stalls offering seeds, nuts, boiled eggs and noodles in broth.

CHUXIONG

The one main stop between Kunming and Xiaguan is in Chuxiong, the centre and administrative capital of Yunnan's Yi minority. A new toll road between Kunming and Chuxiong was completed in 1994 cutting the journey between these two cities down to two and a half hours. At the numerous restaurants and noodle stalls near the bus stop, passengers rush for a quick, filling lunch or night snack before piling back into the bus for the remaining trip. Chuxiong itself is really only a building site at the moment with little to see though this may not be the case for long; developers are planning to turn the town into a tourist attraction. In any case there is little time to explore and you will be extremely unpopular with passengers and the irate bus driver if you show up late. The Kunming-Chengdu railway line is 85 kilometres (53 miles) northwest of Chuxiong.

The bus route from Chuxiong to Dali is almost continuously mountainous, except in the broad Changyun Plain. Here, on one of Yunnan's rare flat, fertile areas, Bronze-Age farmers once thrived. Changyun has an airstrip that played an important role in the fight against the Japanese during World War II. A mountain bulwark rises from the plain, the last great obstacle before entering the Dali Bai Autonomous Region. The bus creeps zigzag fashion up precipitous Red Rocky Mountains, offering a superb view. The road finally levels off before reaching the city of Xiaguan, now known formally as Dali City (Dali Shi).

Buses leave Kunming for Dali several times every morning, the earliest ones departing at six am, and each evening. Tickets can be bought through CITS and other travel agencies or directly from the Passenger Transport Bus Station (Qiche Keyun Zhan) near the train station at the southern end of Beijing Lu. Large buses are preferable to minibuses; they are more comfortable and the drivers (generally) more careful. Special buses with sleeping berths depart each night as well. Taxis can also be hired for the fast eight-hour trip but be prepared to pay up to Rmb 800–1000.

Xiaguan, Yunnan's second largest city, has a population of over 500,000. It spreads around the southwestern tip of Erhai Lake and rises part way up the sur-

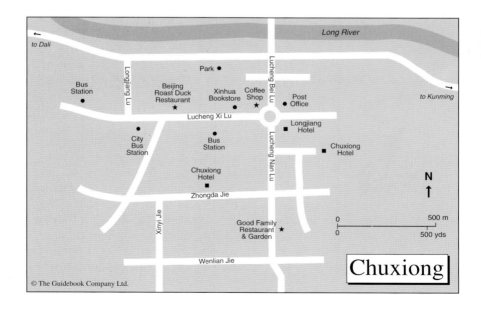

© The Guidebook Company Ltd.

rounding hills. In contrast to small, charming Dali, 15 kilometres (9 miles) to the north, Xiaguan has a good deal of ugly industrial sprawl and little outstanding architecture. It is the main commercial and transportation centre of western Yunnan and all buses make a stop here.

Remarkable changes in Yunnan's transportation have come with the opening of an airport at Xiaguan, to the southeast of the city. Daily jet flights between Dali and Kunming take less than an hour since Dali airport got up and running towards the end of 1995.

An extension of the rail line westward to Xiaguan is underway as well, and is due to be opened in the near future.

Food and Drink in Dali

Because of Xiaguan's large Muslim population, many of the restaurants are halal, offering a good, simple fare of noodles, flat bread, mutton, beancurd and fried vegetables. A number of restaurants can be found in the northern part of the city and along Cangshan Xi Lu. Local specialities are *erkuai,* a noodle-like dish made from pressed rice, usually fried with green onions, and dog, euphemistically known in this part of Yunnan as *diyang,* or 'earth goat'. The earth goat can be missed, but one really should try the dairy products known as *rushan* and *rubing,* the former folded, brittle, fan-shaped cheese, sometimes referred to as fried milk, the latter a mild, soft, white goat's cheese, often fried with beans.

The eating scene in Dali has changed drastically over the years as local entrepreneurs have catered to the tastes of foreigners. Many small restaurants have sprung up with menus in English—most of these cluster near or in front of the Red Camellia Hotel.

Sights in the Dali Region

DALI PREFECTURAL MUSEUM (DALI ZHOU BOWUGUAN)
Open 8.30–11.30 am, 2–5.30 pm, closed Sunday

Sometimes referred to as the Xiaguan museum, this imposing institution with high roofs and yellow tiles is well worth an hour's visit. It stands in Xiaguan's northeast sector near the approach to Erhai Park and is somewhat difficult to find on foot. The entrance faces north.

The museum presents in a series of rooms the material culture, art history, archi-

Fishing Village, Erhai Lake

tecture and ethnic variety of Dali Prefecture's 12 counties.

Room 1 displays neolithic tools and pottery, a bronze axe and moulds for casting. A photograph shows famous Feilong Qiao (Flying Dragon Bridge) spanning the Mekong River in Yunlong County. Here, too, is a precious Warring States (475–221 BC) bronze drum with a distinct, simple star on top, and nearby Han-Dynasty coins and tomb bricks.

Room 2 is devoted to the Nanzhao and Dali Kingdoms. An instructive map shows the greatest extent of the Nanzhao Kingdom, when it dominated virtually all of Yunnan, a part of Sichuan and western Guizhou, northern Laos, a small piece of Thailand and all of eastern Burma far to the north, near present-day Putao. Displays show pagoda bricks with inscriptions, mirrors, shells, bronze *dorjes* (ritual thunderbolts), Song-Dynasty ceramic elephant-dragons from Tianjing Village and many photos of archaeological finds and cultural objects.

Room 3 is made up largely of replicas of the Buddhist caves at Shibaoshan in Jianchuan County (see page 122) and holds large reproduction paintings of the 11th-century Tiannan Guibao, a painted scroll, and scenes from the year 899 of animals, people, teachers and Buddhist objects.

Room 4 has some fine pottery, curious, flattened Ming-Dynasty stone carvings from Jianchuan, tomb figurines and miscellaneous objects and photos.

Room 5 displays the history of 20th-century revolution in Dali and Yunnan, Room 6 is given over to marble and Room 7 is the Folk Customs Hall that presents the 14 different minority groups represented in Dali Prefecture and objects from their lives.

TEA FACTORY (CHACHANG)

Its main task is to supply tea to Tibet and the other distant border regions of China. Yunnan tea is especially prized and 80 per cent of this factory's annual production of 1,600 tons ends up in Tibet where the people drink prodigious amounts of tea for hydration, energy, digestion and hospitality.

For ease in transport and barter and to prevent spoilage the tea is steam-pressed into quarter-kilo bricks. This pressed tea (*jin cha*) was formerly made into enormous two-kilo and four kilo bricks; these can now only be seen in the factory's museum. Other exhibits include a dozen major types of tea products and marvellous 'special issue' bricks embossed in Chinese, English and Russian, which were produced up to the 1970s.

In recent times, the factory has exported tea to Europe. Small, bell-shaped bricks of quality tea, called *tuocha*, have gained great popularity because of the apparent efficacy as a weight reducer. *Tuocha* also claims to 'melt' cholesterol.

NB: The Yunnan Fragrant Flower Tea Factory is closed to foreigners as of spring 1995.

MOSQUE (QINGZHENSI)

Xiaguan's main mosque stands at the end of Wenming Jie in the old part of town west of Renmin Lu. The streets here are small, on a human scale, and the houses rarely more than two storeys. Their handsome wooden exteriors are painted red-brown, or green, and retain the atmosphere of a hundred years ago.

The mosque itself, Xiaguan Qingzhensi, stands beyond a stone and marble entrance gate, beyond a courtyard. Enter respectfully and you will be greeted and welcomed by the residents—several families live within the compound and care for the site and the religious needs of the community. Most families in this part of town are Hui (Chinese Muslims)

ERHAI PARK (ERHAI GONGYUAN)

Xiaguan's most attractive park stretches along Tuanshan Hill at the southern end of Erhai Lake. Royal deer belonging to the Nanzhao kings used to graze here 1,200 years ago, and on a clear day it is easy to see why the spot was chosen for a modern park. The view looks directly up the lake for miles. To the west, fading away majestically, all 19 peaks of the Cangshan range are visible.

The park is well-kept, dotted with pavilions, staircases and flower gardens, and it has a teahouse. A small but meticulously maintained botanical garden lies at the eastern base of the hill, reached by a long descending flight of stairs. Its outstanding collection of camellias, magnolias and azaleas gives an idea of the botanical riches that are native to the Cangshan Mountains. Sometimes fishing fleets of 20 or 30 boats are pulled up at the base of Tuanshan Hill, giving visitors a chance to stop and make friends with the lake dwellers

ERHAI LAKE

The great Erhai, blessing and bane of the Dali Plain, is a constant fixture in the consciousness of the Bai people. It is deep and full of fish. Predictable winds blow from the north in the morning and change direction at day's end, filling the sails of the wooden boats transporting quarry stones, fish, livestock, fodder or wood around the shores. But the lake has another face that is far less benign. Heavy rains can bring devastating floods. Today, dams and predictions from provincial weather stations help to avert disasters.

There are innumerable ways to enjoy the lake—walking along the shore or hiring boats to explore islands and inlets. It is said that the waters are infested with the schistosomiasis parasite (which causes an infestation of blood flukes in the body). It is therefore unsafe to swim.

Three main islands and several temples and villages along the lake's dry eastern shore are worth visiting. About an hour by boat from Xiaguan is Golden Shuttle Island (Jinsuo Dao), with a small fishing community on the east side and a cave for exploring. On the shore, directly north of the island, is a rocky peninsula crowned by a pavilion and temple. Sacred Buddhist buildings, destroyed and rebuilt many times, have stood on this spot for nearly 1,500 years. Luoyuan Temple was badly damaged during the Cultural Revolution but has been put back together and has great charm. Visitors can have their fortunes told by an old priest who guides them in shaking and selecting a single bamboo stick from a bundle of 100. The numbered stick corresponds to a specific fortune.

Much farther up the lake sits a tiny, picturesque temple island, Xiao Putuo Dao, dating from the 15th century. It is devoted to Guanyin, the Goddess of Mercy. The outside walls have been restored with paintings of birds, animals and flowers and the fanciful roof with pointed eaves is especially nice. On the shore nearby is the fishing village of Haiyin, whose boatmen are steeped in the lore of the lake. One of their specialities is night fishing for the huge 40-kilogram (88-pound) 'green fish'.

Near the northern end of Erhai is the village of Tianshengyin and the twin islets of Chiwen Dao and Yuji Dao, a beautiful grouping with old buildings and a pagoda. Sometimes it is possible to catch a boat from here across the lake to Shangguan, near Butterfly Spring, and then ride a bus home to Dali or Xiaguan.

THREE PAGODAS OF DALI (DALI SANTA)

Standing below Lanfeng Peak, slightly to the northwest of Dali Old Town, are three elegant pagodas, known as Chongsheng Santa, the Three Pagodas of Saintly Worship. The outstanding landmarks of the region, they were once part of the greatest temple complex on the Dali plain. The Chongsheng Temple itself has long since disappeared and now only the towers remain. Note: In recent times the Three Pagodas site has become extremely popular with tourists, the inevitable result being that it is overrun with stalls selling marble wares.

The tallest pagoda, named Qianxunta, measures nearly 70 metres (230 feet). It was constructed about 850 under the guidance of three engineers from Chang'an (modern Xi'an), capital of the Tang Dynasty, and is similar in many ways to the Small Wild Goose Pagoda in that city. It has 16 tiers. The two smaller pagodas, each with ten tiers and standing 42 metres (135 feet) high, were built 200 years later and have characteristics of architecture from the Chinese Southern Song (1127–1279).

Pagodas are among the most ubiquitous structures throughout the Buddhist world. Their Sanskrit name is *stupa*, originally a mound or round dome or cylinder on a square base with a shaft emerging upward.

Stupas probably evolved in India from prehistoric times as burial mounds for

(Opposite) Qianxunta, the finest pagoda on the Dali Plain

Speak of the Devil

*I*n the morning we had another beautiful walk round the snow-clad mountains to the village of Yangpi, at the back of Tali. There was a long delay here. News of my arrival spread, and the people hurried along to see me. No sooner was I seated at an inn than two messengers from the yamen called for my passport. They were officious young fellows, sadly wanting in respect, and they asked for my passport in a noisy way that I did not like, so I would not understand them. I only smiled at them in the most friendly manner possible. I kept them for some time in a fever of irritation at their inability to make me understand; I listened with imperturbable calmness to their excited phrases till they were nearly dancing. Then I leisurely produced my passport, as if to satisfy a curiosity of my own, and began scanning it. Seeing this, they rudely thrust forth their hands to seize it; but I had my eye on them. "Not so quick, my friends," I said, soothingly. "Be calm, nervous irritability is a fruitful source of trouble. See, here is my passport; here is the official seal, and here the name of your unworthy servant. Now I fold it up carefully—put it back in my pocket. But here is a copy, which is at your service. If you wish to show the original to the magistrate, I will take it to his honour myself, but out of my hands it does not pass." They looked puzzled, as they did not understand English; they debated a minute or two, and then went away with the copy, which in due time they politely returned to me.

If you wish to travel quickly in China, never be in a hurry. Appear unconscious of all that is passing; never be irritated by any delay, and assume complete indifference, even when you are really anxious to push on. Emulate, too, that leading trait in the Chinese character, and never understand anything which you do not wish to understand. No man on earth can be denser than a Chinaman, when he chooses. Let me give an instance. It was not so long ago, in a police court in Melbourne, that a

Chinaman was summoned for being in possession of a tenement unfit for human habitation. The case was clearly proved, and he was fined £1. But in no way could John be made to understand that a fine had been inflicted. He sat there with unmoved stolidity, and all that the court could extract from him was: "My no savvy, no savvy." After saying this in a voice devoid of all hope, he sank again into silence. Here rose a well-known lawyer. "With your worship's permission, I think I can make the Chinaman understand," he said. He was permitted to try. Striding fiercely up to the poor Celestial, he said to him, in a loud voice, "John, you are fined two pounds." "No dam fear! Only one!"

Rarely during my journey to Burma was I offended by hearing myself called "Yang kweitze" (foreign devil), although this is the universal appellation of the foreigner wherever Mandarin is spoken in China. To-day, however, (May 6th), I was seated at the inn in the town of Chutung when I heard the offensive term. I was seated at a table in the midst of the accustomed crowd of Chinese. I was on the highest seat, of course, because I was the most important person present, when a bystander, seeing that I spoke no Chinese, coolly said the words "Yang kweitze' (foreign devil). I rose in my wrath, and seized my whip. "You Chinese devil"(Chung kweitze), I said in Chinese, and then I assailed him in English. He seemed surprised at my warmth, but said nothing, and, turning on his heel, walked uncomfortably away.

I often regretted afterwards that I did not teach the man a lesson, and cut him across the face with my whip; yet, had I done so, it would have been unjust. He called me, as I thought, "Yang kweitze," but I have no doubt, having told the story to Mr. Warry, the Chinese adviser to the Government of Burma, that he did not use these words at all, but others so closely resembling them that they sounded identically the same to my untrained ear, and yet signified not "foreign devil," but "honoured guest." He had paid me a compliment; he had not insulted me. The Yunnanese, Mr. Warry tells me, do not readily speak of the devil for fear he should appear.

G.E. Morrison, *An Australian in China*, 1895

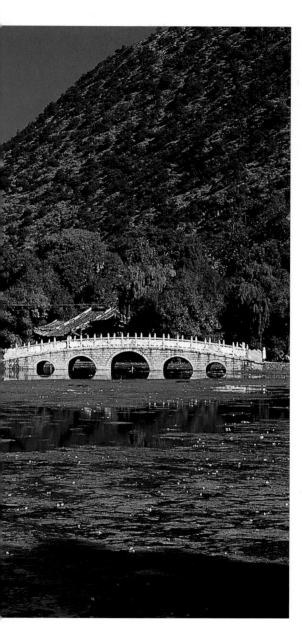

Moon-Embracing Pavilion at Black Dragon Pond in Lijiang with Jade Dragon Snow Mountain (Yulongxue Shan) in background

local rulers and heroes. Legend says that in the fifth century BC Shakyamuni, the historical Buddha, asked to have his ashes interred in a stupa. Since that time stupas have become symbols of the Buddha, reminders of his earthly existence, cult objects and places of devotion.

As Buddhism spread through Asia the shape of stupas adapted itself to local architecture, giving rise to the huge variety of styles. Generally speaking there are three types of stupas, or pagodas, in China.

The Storeyed style: This results from traditional Chinese storeyed architecture and is marked by panoramic views from large windows and outer railings at each level.

The Pavilion style: This is also known as the 'single-layered stupa', with one storey only.

The Close-eaved or (**Miyi**) **style**, or multi-eaved style: These pagodas are characterized by a spacious first storey, low subsequent storeys and all eaves spaced closely to one another. Windows are small or nonexistent and the interior space is cramped and dark. Close-eaved pagodas are an early style whose popularity rested on the extreme simplicity and gracefulness of form. They are best viewed from a distance where their lines can be seen in relief against a mountain or the far horizon.

The Chongsheng Santa are clearly of the third type, as are nearly all remaining pagodas on the Dali plain. They were built by the 'earth stacking method', whereby terraces of earth were constructed around the pagoda as it rose storey by storey. The immense outer structure of dirt, functioning as a scaffolding, was finally removed to reveal the finished masterpiece.

The pagodas were founded for two main reasons. First, they were holy structures that invoked the Buddha's protection against the frequent disasters of floods and earthquakes. A carved marble inscription in front of Qianxunta bears the four Chinese characters *yong zhen shan chuan*, Subdue Forever the Mountains and the Rivers. Secondly, the pagodas were reliquaries for the ashes and bones of saints and a storehouse for scriptures and precious objects. During reconstruction work in 1979 a priceless hoard of 400 objects—statues, paintings, sutras, jewels, unguents and medicines, copper mirrors, gold and silver ornaments, utensils and musical instruments—was discovered in the roof of Qianxunta pagoda. A small museum behind the pagodas recounts their history.

DALI CITY MUSEUM
Located in the south part of the old town of Dali, just off the main street, this well-kept, well-presented museum has few displays but contains some treasures.

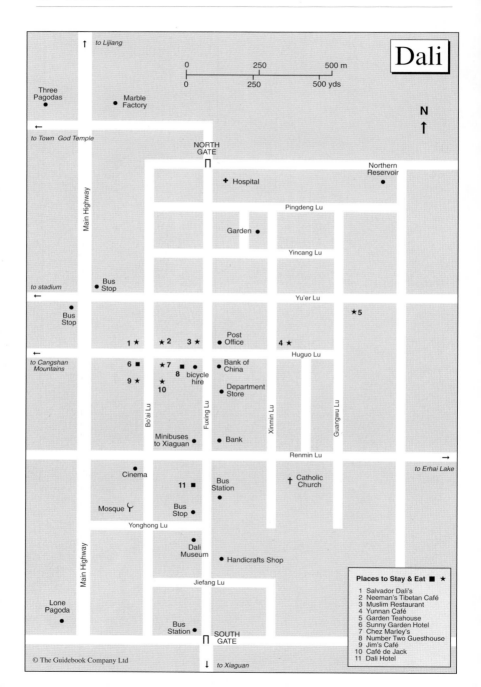

to Lijiang

Three
Pagodas

Marble
Factory

Dali

0   250   500 m
0   250   500 yds

N

to Town God Temple

NORTH
GATE

Northern
Reservoir

Main Highway

+ Hospital

Pingdeng Lu

Garden

Yincang Lu

to stadium

Bus
Stop

Yu'er Lu

Bus
Stop

★5

to Cangshan
Mountains

1 ★   ★2   3 ★

Post
Office

4 ★

Huguo Lu

6 ■   ★7

8 ■

bicycle
hire

Bank of
China

9 ★   ★
10

Department
Store

Bo'ai Lu

Fuxing Lu

Xinmin Lu

Guangwu Lu

Minibuses
to Xiaguan

Bank

Renmin Lu

to Erhai Lake

Cinema

11 ■

Bus
Station

† Catholic
Church

Mosque ⛎

Bus
Stop

Yonghong Lu

Main Highway

Dali
Museum

Handicrafts Shop

Jiefang Lu

Lone
Pagoda

Bus
Station

SOUTH
GATE

© The Guidebook Company Ltd

to Xiaguan

Places to Stay & Eat ■ ★

1 Salvador Dali's
2 Neeman's Tibetan Café
3 Muslim Restaurant
4 Yunnan Café
5 Garden Teahouse
6 Sunny Garden Hotel
7 Chez Marley's
8 Number Two Guesthouse
9 Jim's Café
10 Café de Jack
11 Dali Hotel

The centrepiece on the ground floor is a large, horizontal, topographic map of Erhai Lake and the Dali region. It is useful as an aid in memorizing the area's geography—it has 48 numbered entries (in Chinese only) that identify major cultural sites. In this room also are neolithic potsherds and axe heads, Spring and Autumn Period (770–476 BC) bronze swords, hoes and axes, Han Dynasty (206 BC–220 AD) weapons and pottery and, from the site of Dazhatuo, a remarkable bronze stand and lamp on a strange pedestal. A central pole supports branch-like decorations that sprout coins like fruit (a money tree?) and below a dragon-reptile resembling a thecodont curves its long neck and fierce head.

From the Nanzhao and Dali Kingdoms (738–1253) are cowrie shells, roof tiles with decorations, a pagoda brick from Hongshengsi Temple with Brahmi script, bronze bodhisattvas from Sheli Pagoda and *dorjes* (ritual bronze thunderbolts) with finger ring holders. From Fotu Pagoda (see below) are more *dorjes* and miniature pagodas. Backing the displays is a reproduction of the Nanzhao Scroll and finally there sits a 10th-century stone Buddha with mustache and excellent eyebrows.

Upstairs are a number of outstanding bronze mirrors. Those from the Song Dynasty (960–1279) are particularly interesting, with images of sage, crane, acolyte, trigrams and tortoise. Large seals were once used by the Ming-Dynasty garrison at Dali.

The main glass exhibition cases display six wooden sculptures: the Four Guardian Kings (*tianwang*) and the bodhisattvas Samantabhadra (Puxian) and Manjushri (Wenshu). These figures, each standing one metre (3 feet), are first-rate pieces of religious art that date from the Yuan Dynasty (1279–1368); they comprise some of the little wooden sculpture to survive from that era. These pieces were carved in Jianchuan County to the north of Dali and are typical of that regional style. Manjushri rides a lion, Samantabhadra an elephant. Both wear spectacular crown-headdresses and rest their feet on lotus-stirrups. All six statues were once gilded.

Other displays in the large upstairs room include cremation jars from the Yuan and Ming, stone rubbings related to the death ritual and dozens of ceramic tomb figurines, many of them lively, colourful and humourous. Court ladies carry games, goods, offerings, a whisk, a *guzheng* (a Chinese zither). Cavaliers, bards, musicians and dancers proclaim the good life after death.

A row of zodiacal and mythical animals—a friendly dragon, a disgruntled tortoise, a chicken waiting to lay an egg, a bored dog—are whimsical and wonderful in their expressiveness. They date from the Ming Dynasty (1368–1644).

Behind the main museum building, in a back courtyard, are exhibitions of Ming and Qing pottery, cut and polished marble and a 'forest of steles' (*beilin*) with many Yuan and Ming steles that are valuable for scholars.

CATHOLIC AND PROTESTANT CHURCHES

Dali's Catholic church (*tianzhujiao tang*) stands at No.6 Xinmin Lu, just off Renmin Lu. It was built in 1938 and is an odd mixture of Chinese architecture and Western religious motifs. The damp interior has a marble altar, plastic flowers, kitsch posters but a beautiful ceiling of gold stars and suns painted on a blue background. The exterior of the main door has some fine wood carving, including the depiction of seminaries far away. The mood of the place, situated inside a compound with a small garden, is quite melancholy.

The Protestant Church of Christ (*jidujiao hui*) at No. 576 Fuxing Lu was first set up in 1913, though the present stark and simple structure, with huge beams and a box-like interior, is not the original. A bell from that former church is rung on Sunday mornings. Protestant missionaries first came to Dali in 1881 to spread the Gospel. Later they established a hospital, renowned throughout the area, that was staffed by English and American doctors.

PUXIAN TEMPLE

To reach this small temple, go east down Yu'er Lu nearly to the edge of town and turn left onto a dirt path at a sign that marks 'Qingshiqiao'.

Puxian Si was established in 1586 and underwent major renovations in 1677, 1854 and in the 1980s. The eaves and roof are valuable remnants, as are the supporting columns at the far left and right of the main building's front facade.

DALI MARBLE FACTORY (DALISHI CHANG)

There are over 30 large marble factories throughout China but this is the most famous. Small wonder considering the Chinese word for marble is *dalishi* (Dali stone). Marble of the finest quality has been quarried here for 1,200 years and the great scars high up on the faces of Cangshan have only begun to eat into a supply that will last for millennia.

The factory, on the northern outskirts of Dali, was set up in 1956 and most of its employees have ancestors who were marble workers. Products are made from a choice of four kinds of marble: 'pure white', 'coloured flower', 'cloud grey' and 'handicraft marble'. It is fascinating to see giant slicing machines slowly cutting through five-ton blocks of marble, a process that takes two or three days. Each year, vast amounts of marble are prepared—most is sent to Canton for export to Hong Kong, Japan and throughout Southeast Asia.

Marble carvings and statuary abound throughout the markets of Dali, though most of the wares are not to the taste of foreigners, being either too kitsch or too heavy. With time and a discerning eye, however, some really worthy marble objects can be found. Thinly sliced discs or fan-shaped pieces of marble, polished but uncarved, sometimes have a natural grain resembling a classical Chinese mountain landscape.

NANZHAO STELE (NANZHAO DEHUA BEI) AND TAIHE RUINS

The Nanzhao Stele, also known by its formal name of Nanzhao Dehua Bei (Nanzhao Sinicization Stele), is an historically important stone tablet from the year 766. It records the offices of a bureaucracy under the Nanzhao Kingdom, describes the economic and political system and specifies the distribution of people within the realm. More important, it recounts Nanzhao's on-again, off-again alliances with the Tang Dynasty.

The stele, a time-pocked black monolith 3 metres (10 feet) tall, stands in a pavilion halfway between Dali and Xiaguan on the rising slopes of the plain, above the main road. It is between the Cangshan range's Shengying and Foding peaks.

This site was formerly within the city walls of Taihe, Nanzhao's first capital; remnants of its walls appear as long mounds on the hillsides. The Old Nanzhao Highway can still be seen nearby as a shallow furrow running away to the north.

The Nanzhao Stele was accidentally rediscovered, copied and studied by a Qing-Dynasty scholar at the end of the 18th century. Were it not for him, the carved characters and the history they tell would have been lost. Much of the writing has indeed been obliterated, worn away by time and pilfered through the centuries by people seeking pieces of the stele to grind into powder for medicine.

SNAKE BONE PAGODA (SHEGUTA)

The dragon, one of China's most complex mythological symbols, has one manifestation whereby it rules over springs, lakes and water courses. Dragons were frequently blamed for the flooding of Erhai Lake and pagodas were erected for protection from the scaly monsters. Snake Bone Pagoda was built to commemorate a brave young man who died while vanquishing one of these 'dragons', which in fact turned out to be a large python, a perfect surrogate and scapegoat. The common people burned the devil snake and buried its bones under the pagoda.

Snake Bone Pagoda is similar in form to Qianxunta, stands over 30 metres (98 feet) tall and was built at the end of the ninth century. The pagoda was a part of the Fotu Temple complex (destroyed) and as such is formally known as Fotusita. It is located under Xieyang Peak, 4 kilometres (2.5 miles) northwest of Xiaguan.

BUTTERFLY SPRING (HUDIEQUAN)

This prosaic site in no way approaches its high reputation, and today, with its aggressive, overcrowded market and hordes of gawping tourists, one can say it is repulsive. But by hiking under the last of Cangshan's 19 peaks and exploring the northern end of Erhai Lake, a visit here can be turned to good advantage.

The legend of Butterfly Spring tells how this spot was a tryst for two young lovers of the Bai nationality. They were happy beyond words but, tragically, hidebound social rules, inflexible elders and persecution drove them to a double suicide. Ever since, they have re-emerged each spring as a pair of butterflies, accompanied by their mascot companion, a golden deer, which now appears as a small, yellow butterfly.

The spring, in a shady grove on the lower slopes of the Cangshan, was justifiably famous for centuries because of a breathtaking convergence every springtime of tens of thousands of butterflies at this spot. The phenomenon was documented many times. Alas, since the mass introduction of insecticides in 1958, the numbers have steadily diminished and the spectacle no longer occurs.

Butterfly Spring lies just off the main road, 35 kilometres (22 miles) north of Dali. The spring itself forms a clear pool and the hills above afford a fine view of the lake.

ZHOUCHENG AND XIZHOU VILLAGES

These two villages, containing some first-rate architecture, still carry on the unspoilt daily rhythm of life on the Dali plain. Zhoucheng Village lies near Butterfly Spring, 30 kilometres (19 miles) north of Dali on the main road. Its inhabitants are nearly pure Bai, with only 50 of its 1,500 households belonging to non-Bai people (Han, Naxi and Dai). Zhoucheng rests below Yunlong Peak and has achieved considerable wealth through its dynamic agriculture and diversified industries. In recent years the locals have set about producing confectionery, noodles, liquor, toys and tie-dyed cloth. There is a boom in house building as well. The solid construction, attention to detail, roofing and stone masonry are all impressive.

Two giant fig trees (*Ficus stipulata*) stand in the main market square, a place where young and old gather to buy and sell produce, meet with friends, swap stories and enjoy themselves. Every Bai village tries to maintain such trees for beauty, shade and blessing.

Xizhou Village has a more mixed population and cosmopolitan background. It grew and flourished in the Ming Dynasty (1368–1644) along with the fortunes of Dali's renowned tea merchants. Each year enormous trains of pack animals would set out from Xiaguan loaded with bricks of tea for the thirsty markets of Tibet. This lucrative trade spawned a class of financiers and agents who in time gathered in Xizhou to build their gardens and pleasure-houses. Although sadly run-down, many of these eccentric structures remain, including a French *fin de siècle* mansion.

Xizhou is also famous for producing carved doors and staircases, which can be seen for sale on market days up and down the Dali plain. The village lies 3 kilometres (1.8 miles) east of the main north-south road; the turn-off is 20 kilometres (12.5 miles) north of Dali, just before the bridge over Wanhua Stream. Farther down a side road beyond Xizhou lies the protected port of Haishe in a serene lakeside setting of spits, promontories, islets and inlets. A hotel in Xizhou is a good place to stay for a few quiet days, away from the crowds of Xiaguan and Dali to the south.

OTHER SIGHTS

The Dali Plain, with a long and florid history, is dotted here and there with miscellaneous cultural sites and tumbledown ruins. Listed below are some less well-known places that can form part of a day trip from either Xiaguan or Dali.

Around Xiaguan are the Confucian Temple, Han Dynasty Tomb, Wanren Tomb and Gantong Temple. Slightly to the northwest lies Jiangjun Temple, erected to honour General Li Mi, a Tang emissary who fought against the Dali Kingdom (936–1253).

The Dali city wall and gate tower were built during the Ming Dynasty (1368–1644). The gate tower, known as the Tower of Five Glories, was one of the finest in all China, far outshining in splendour the present 1984 reconstruction.

Near Dali, beyond the town's southwest corner, is Lone Pagoda (Yita), a close-eaves style pagoda built during the tenth century. In any other country this magnificent cultural treasure would be honoured, but here the ground floor has been broken into and the interior used as a toilet.

Farther north, below Zhong He Peak on the grounds of the Dali Fair, stands the Kublai Khan Memorial Stele, a huge 4.4-metre (14-foot) inscribed tablet formed by two separate pieces of stone mounted on an enormous turtle. Two styles of calligraphy were used to inscribe more than 1100 characters that praise Kublai Khan's exploits and conquest of Dali in 1253. The date of the inscription is 1304, and the stele is known formally as the Pacification of Yunnan Stele.

The small Goddess of Mercy Temple (Guanyintang) lies 5 kilometres (3 miles) south of Dali. It is built over a great rock which, legend says, was brought there by the goddess herself to block the path of an invading army. This temple has some excellent stone and wood carving.

The tomb of Du Wenxiu (1823–72) lies in the village of Xiadui, a few kilometres southeast of Dali. He was a Muslim from Baoshan District to the west who led a vast uprising between the years 1855 and his death. This is sometimes referred to as the Muslim Uprising, and Du Wenxiu was its leader.

An Account of the Muslim Rebellion (1855–1873)

The Mohammedans of Yunnan are precisely the same race as their Confucian or Buddhist countrymen; and it is even doubtful if they were Mohammedans except as far as they profess an abhorrence for pork. They did not practise circumcision, though I am not sure if that rite is indispensable; and they did not observe the Sabbath, were unacquainted with the language of Islam, did not turn to Mecca in prayer, and professed none of the fire and sword spirit of propogandism.

That they were intelligent, courageous, honest and liberal to strangers, is as certain as their ignorance of the law and the prophets. All honor to their good qualities, but let us cease to cite their short-lived rule as an instance of the 'Great Mohammedan Revival.'

The rebellion was at first a question of pork and of nothing else, beginning with jealousies and bickering between pig butchers and the fleshers of Islam in the market place. The officials who were appealed to invariably decided against the Mussulmans. Great discontent ensued and soon burst into flame.

The first outbreak seemed to have originated among the miners, always a dangerous class in China, who were largely composed of Mohammedans. The usual measures of exterminative repression were adopted by the officials; their Confucian hostility against any faith or society which possessed an organization novel to or discountenanced by the Government, was aroused; a general persecution ensued; the Mohammedans made common cause, excited, it is very possible, by their travelled hadjis; and so began the period of disorder and disaster with which we are acquainted.

The commander of our Chinese escort—whose name, by the way, ... is not inappropriate to his profession, 'Hill-echoing Thunder'—narrated to us how he conveyed with exceeding difficulty four foreign guns over the rugged route from Yunnan Fu (Kunming), and how the capture of the city was to be attributed solely to his own exertions. One gun was irreparably damaged en route, but the surviving three laid and pointed by himself, according to his account, terminated the rebellion. There seems no doubt that these guns, cast by French workmen in Kunming, were really the main cause of the Mohammedan surrender.

General Thunder told us, what was subsequently confirmed, that when the Mohammedans had surrendered and given up their arms, Tu Wen-hsiu, the so-called 'sultan', and came into the camp of the beseigers, borne in a sedan chair, and inquired for Ma, the Imperialist commander. Being introduced to his presence, he begged for a cup of water, which being given him, he said, 'I have nothing to ask but this—spare the people.' He then drank the water, and almost immediately expired. It appears that he had taken poison, which was suddenly brought into action by the water. His head was immediately cut off and exposed, and, heedless of his prayer—probably the most impressive and pathetic ever uttered by a dying patriot—the victors proceeded to massacre the helpless garrison and townsfolk.

The greater part of the able-bodied men, no doubt retaining some of their arms, succeeded in escaping; but a number of unresisting people, principally old men, women and children, fled from the city into the rice fields that border the lake. Hemmed in by the Imperialist pursuers, they entered the water, into which they retreated further and further; and being still pressed, were either forced out of their depth by the crush, or sought a refuge from worse ills in a voluntary death. The number of those who perished in the way has probably been greatly exaggerated. The foreign press puts it at from 3,000 to 9,000. General Thunder, undoubtedly an eye-witness, and probably a participator, told me, as we sat in the sunny verandah of a temple overlooking the scene of these horrors, that he did not think there could have been more than 500 corpses, or 'the water would have stunk more.' The gallant general was of the opinion that Tu Wen-hsiu was a good and conscientious ruler, and respected even by his Imperialist foes; but for the Muslims generally, he professed much contempt.

Grosvenor, Parliamentary Report: Mission Through Western
Yunnan, China, No. 3 (1878)

At the far northern end of Erhai Lake, beyond Butterfly Spring, lies the village of Shaping, host to a lively, colourful market each Monday. There is a small hotel here. Boats from Caicun to Wase on the eastern shore leave each afternoon. Wase has a guesthouse, and a market every Saturday. Shuanglang, at the far northeast end of Erhai Lake, is a bucolic village with a Sunday market.

A number of lesser temples dot the eastern slopes of the Cangshan Range. Going north from the foothills above Dali, they are Zhonghe Temple, Wuwei Temple, Shengyuan Temple and Luocha Pavilion.

Sights Beyond Dali

CHICKEN FOOT MOUNTAIN (JIZUSHAN)

Northeast of Dali in Binchuan County's Liandong district stands Jizushan, a high, sacred mountain that rises 3,220 metres (10,562 feet). It has been an important pilgrimage site and monastic centre for both Buddhists and Daoists since the seventh century. The mountain gets its peculiar name from the configuration of the entire range, which is made up of three separate ridges in front and one in back, thus forming the shape of a giant chicken's foot. It can be reached by taking a bus from Xiaguan to Binchuan, a distance of 70 kilometres (44 miles), and then carrying on another 24 kilometres (15 miles) to the Bai village of Shazhi at Jizushan's base.

The long walk up is amply rewarded by the view from the summit. The mountain's isolation and splendid position between Erhai Lake and the upper reaches of the Yangzi River have frequently been praised by poets:

Sunrise in the East
Cangshan's nineteen peaks in the West
Snow to the North
Endless hills and clouds to the South

This holy mountain, once alive with over 360 temples and hermitages and 3,000 monks, was systematically attacked by Red Guards in the late 1960s, purportedly to end superstition, alchemy and madness. Every major site was damaged or destroyed and only now have some of the pieces been put back together. Even so it is impossible to hope or imagine that Jizushan will ever come close to recreating its formidable past when representatives from Buddhist countries all over Asia came here to live. Weather-beaten Tibetans arrived regularly after travelling the pilgrim road for months or years. On this mountain the diverse theologies of Theravada,

Mahayana and Tantric Buddhism mingled freely in one place.

Sacred Wish (Zhusheng) was the central temple on the mountain. It honoured the monk Jiaye who came from India to spread Buddhism. Legend recounts how Jiaye established Buddhism on Jizushan by mastering magical forces and overcoming the wicked Chicken Foot King in titanic battles. Zhusheng Temple was renowned for its bronze statuary and two enormous brass cauldrons, each capable of holding enough rice to feed 1,000 people.

Mid-mountain Temple (Zhongshan Si) lies half way up and has a community of monks. This is a good place for tea and a rest on the ascent. Huashoumen gate and temple did largely survive the Cultural Revolution and mark the beginning of the steep climb to the top.

The walk up the mountain leads through remnants of famous walnut forests that once supplied Dali with house beams and wood for the coffins of the rich. The top of the mountain is called Heavenly Pillar Peak (Tianzhu Feng) and nearby on a precipice, known as Golden Summit (Jin Ding), is the crowning spire, Lenyan Pagoda. It is a square, close-eaves style pagoda with 13 storeys that rises 40 metres (130 feet) above the summit (altitude 3240 metres). It was probably first built in the 11th century and has remained the symbol of Jizushan despite all the devastation.

STONE TREASURE MOUNTAIN BUDDHIST CAVES (SHIBAOSHAN SHIKU)

China is rich in Buddhist cave centres. Most notable among these are Bezeklik and Kizil in Xinjiang, Dunhuang and Maijishan in Gansu Province, Yungang in Shanxi Province, Longmen in Henan Province and Dazu in Sichuan Province. The Stone Treasure Mountain caves, though less extensive than these, are Yunnan's finest, a complex of three main sites carved and constructed primarily in the ninth century. They are in a remote mountain region 130 kilometres (81 miles) north of Dali by road in Jianchuan County. Follow the main highway towards Lijiang as far as the village of Diannan, eight kilometres (five miles) before Jianchuan. There is a complicated intersection here. As you turn left (west), be sure to stay on the road that angles back towards the southwest. Do not go in the direction of Yangling. Rather, follow the southwest road for 16 kilometres (10 miles) until you find a conspicuous stone marker next to the main road. This is the entrance to the cave complex by way of a dirt road. The main group of caves is carved into a cliff face at Stone Bell Mountain (Shizhong Shan) above Stone Bell Temple, some eight kilometres (five miles) beyond this turn-off.

Apart from fine depictions Buddhist deities and disciples, these caves are out-

Logging is a major industry in many parts of Yunnan. Here in the northwest, loggers gather at a roadhead to begin loading timber onto trucks for the long four-day trip to Kunming

standing for their presentation of life under the Nanzhao Kingdom. The works are entirely carvings, with no frescoes. Statues of foreigners with aquiline noses, beards and high brows indicate distant contacts through trade and diplomacy. Habits, clothing and customs of the Nanzhao royal family are shown in vivid detail. Grotto Number One at Stone Bell Mountain holds nine imperial figures with one seated amidst the others; he wears a long, elaborate gown. This is King Yi Mouxun (reigned 779–808), under whose rule Nanzhao increasingly adopted Tang models for political institutions, and borrowed Chinese cultural and literary forms.

Another cave at Stone Bell Temple is known as the Ge Luofeng Grotto. Ge Luofeng was a Nanzhao king as well, 30 years before Yi Mouxun. During his reign Nanzhao forces dealt the Tang armies a series of crushing defeats. This grotto is carefully carved to give the impression of a resplendent hall, with three overlapping tiers.

Certainly the most extraordinary cave is the Grotto of Female Genitalia. Here artists have carried the praise and veneration of fertility to an amazing degree, with a graphic depiction of a 50-centimetre-high (20-inch) vulva.

There are two lesser sites within the entire Stone Treasure Mountain complex. Lion Pass (Shizi Guan), across a small ravine from Stone Bell Temple, has three caves. Grotto Number Two at Lion Pass is historically significant for its carving of a Persian noble. Small caves and carvings near Shadeng Village are spread across a long stretch of mountainous land several kilometres south of Stone Bell Temple.

RAINBOW BRIDGE (JIHONGQIAO)

This iron chain bridge once crossed a deep gorge of the Mekong River (Lancang Jiang) 185 kilometres (115 miles) by road southwest from Xiaguan. Rainbow Bridge is reached by first going westward to Yongping, then travelling southward for 38 kilometres (24 miles) to Changjie (Changgai). After this, continue westward again for 20 kilometres (12.5 miles) to Yonghe and then on to the river.

Although records show iron bridges to have existed in this part of the world since the Eastern Han Dynasty (AD 25–200), Rainbow Bridge is the only one with a continuous history of a thousand years in one location. The bridge was built in 1475 and consisted of 17 iron chains, each chain made up of 176 rings. The length was 60 metres (197 feet) and the width 3.8 metres (12.5 feet). Wooden boards laid across the chains allowed people and animals to cross.

Pavilions and poems carved in the surrounding cliffs attest to the importance of Rainbow Bridge as a vital trade and diplomatic link with India, Burma and Thailand. Distinguished tourists of the past have visited here, including Emperor Kangxi (reigned 1661–1722) and Marco Polo.

BAI TOMBS

Shundang Baishi Township in Yunlong County has a large number of carved stone tombs that constitute a Bai nationality burial ground.

The area contains an ancient brine pit, a source of salt through the centuries. The families who worked it and earned their fortunes from the salt trade were named Yang, Dong, Zhao and Li; the names are still prominent. These owners and managers of the salt wells were buried in the mountainside, and this became the start of the Bai tombs.

The tombs face east towards the rising sun and a river that passes below them. They are made from a local reddish sandstone and all have an arched 'gateway'. At the left and right of the arch are carved stone columns surmounted by lions. Inside are three tablets and four pillars. A main marble tablet bears an inscribed epitaph, those on left and right record the family history and biography of the deceased.

The craftsmen of the tombs took great care in the miniature architecture and design elements. Altars stand in front of the main tablet for offerings; guardians stand as protectors of the tomb; scenes carved in high relief show people enjoying food and games; almost toy-like animals—lion, dragon, deer, elephant, horse, fish in 'water' made with carved, wavy lines—grace the walls and recesses of the tombs.

There is more freedom here than with the more familiar Han tombs, especially in the treatment of humans. They have vivid faces with large, upturned eyes, stylized with swirling hair, beards and moustaches.

WEIBAO SHAN

Sixty-five kilometres south of Dali rises Yunnan's most famous Daoist mountain, Weibao Shan. It stands within the Weishan Yi and Moslem (Hui) Autonomous Region; Weishan is the county seat and point of departure for the mountain. The town is outstanding for its 100-year-old architecture, mosques and markets. Weibao Shan had more that 20 temples before the Cultural Revolution, but now there are only three, although reconstruction continues. It is possible to find peace, quiet and beautiful views on this mountain if you go at the right time (late autumn). If you want company, expect thousands to join you from the first to the fifteenth day of the second lunar month; this is the mountain's annual pilgrim festival.

In Lijiang: Rock's Kingdom

*I*t is a cold, sunny Sunday in Yunnan. On the plain below Jade Dragon Mountain, the villagers of Baisha are letting off fire-crackers to celebrate the building of a house, and the village doctor is holding a feast in his upper room, in honour of his firstborn grandson.

The sun filters through the lattices, bounces off rafters hung with corn-cobs and lights up everyone's faces. Apart from us, almost all the guests are members of the Naxi (Nakhi) tribe.

The Naxi are the descendants of Tibetan nomads who, many centuries ago, exchanged their tents for houses and settled in the Lijiang Valley, to grow rice and buckwheat at an altitude of over 8,000 feet. Their religion was—and surreptitiously still is—a combination of Tibetan Lamaism, Chinese Daoism and a far, far older shamanistic belief: in the spirits of cloud and wind and pine.

The Doctor has seated us, with his four brothers, at the table of honour beside the east window.

Below, along the street, there are lines of weeping willows and a quick-water stream in which some pale brown ducks are playing. Led by the drake, they swim furiously against the current, whiz back down to the bridge and then begin all over again.

The panelled housefronts are painted the colour of ox blood. Their walls are of mud brick, flecked with chaff, and their tiled roofs stretch away, rising and sagging, in the direction of the old dynastic temple of the ancient kings of Mu.

None of the Doctor's brothers look the least bit alike. The most vigorous is a leathery, Mongol-eyed peasant, who keeps refilling my bowl of firewater. The second, with bristly grey hair and a face of smiling wrinkles, sits immobile as a meditating monk. The other two are a tiny man with a wandering gaze and a shadowy presence under a fur-lined hat.

Looking across to the ladies' table, we are amazed by the fullfleshed, dimpled beauty of the young girls and the quiet dignity of the older women. They are all in traditional costume, in the celestial colours—blue and white. Some, it is true, are

Hieroglyphics on a Naxi Dongba manuscript

wearing Mao caps, but most are in a curved blue bonnet, rather like a Flemish coif. Our Shanghai friend, Tsong-Zung, says we might well be guests at Bruegel's 'Peasant Wedding'. Apart from the bonnet, the women's costume consists of a blue bodice, a pleated white apron and a stiff, quilted cape secured with crossbands. Every Naxi woman carries the cosmos on her back: the upper part of the cape is a band of indigo representing the night sky; the lower, a lobe of creamy silk or sheepskin that stands for the light of day. The two halves are separated by a row of seven disks that symbolize the stars—although the sun and moon, once worn on either shoulder, have now gone out of fashion.

Girls come up from the kitchen with the sweet course: apples preserved in honey, melons in ginger, sour plums in alcohol. More girls then come with the Nine Dishes—the Nine Dragons, as they've been called since the Zhou (Chou) Dynasty: in this case, cubes of pork fat and winter sausage, water chestnuts, lotus root, carp, taros, bean tops, rice fritters, a fungus known as tree ears, and a heap of tripe and antique eggs that go, like sulphur bombs, straight to the gut.

From time to time, the Doctor himself appears at the head of the stairs, in a white clinician's mobcap and silver-grey cotton greatcoat. He surveys the company with the amused, slightly otherworldly air of a Daoist gentleman-scholar, and flicks his wispy beard from side to side. As soon as the meal is over, he appears again, hypodermic in hand, as if to remind us that healing, even on the 'Big Happy Day' is work without end.

The grandson's name is Deshou: 'De' for virtue, 'Shou' for longevity. On a sheet of red paper, now pinned to the porch, the old man has written the following:

The grandfather grants his grandson the name 'Deshou'.
De is high as the Big Dipper.
Shou is like the southern mountain.
De is valued by the world.
Shou is respected by men.
De is an oily rain.
Shou the fertilized field.
Long life and health to him, born 10.30am, 9th Moon, 14th Day.

The focus of all this adoration is swaddled in a length of gold-and-purple Tibetan brocade, and has the face of a man born wise. He is on show downstairs, in his mother's lap. The bedroom has white-papered walls to which are pasted scarlet cut-outs of characters representing happiness and of butterflies flying in pairs.

Apart from the Doctor's herbal and his English dictionary, the swaddling clothes are the family's only treasure to survive the Cultural Revolution, when Red Guards ransacked the house.

The Doctor takes the baby and cradles him in his arms.

'I have plenty,' he says, gesturing to the revellers in the courtyard. 'Six years ago I had nothing. But now I have plenty.' His wife comes from the kitchen and stands beside him. And with her deep blue bonnet, and smile of tender resignation, she reminds us of Martha or Mary in a Florentine altarpiece.

The Red Guards stripped him of everything, and he was forbidden to practise. 'It was she who saved me,' he says. 'Without her I could not have lived.'

Their son, the father of three weeks' standing, is a young man of 27 in a neat blue Chinese suit. He is a self-taught teacher of English, and now also a student of medicine.

Proudly, he shows us his wedding cup—a porcelain bowl painted with peacocks, on which the village calligrapher has added a couplet by the Tang poet Bai Juyi:

One only wishes that people will live forever
And be in couples even at a distance of 1,000 li.

The calligrapher—a courteous, hook-nosed old gentleman— is the Doctor's cousin and also one of the party. He has spent many years, as an ideological bygone, in jail. But now—in this new, relaxed, undoctrinaire China—he has retired to his tiny house by the stream: to practise the arts of seal cutting, brush-work and the culture of orchids. On Tuesday, when we called on him, he showed us a lilac autumn crocus with a label in Chinese reading 'Italian autumn narcissus'.

The Doctor, too, is a passionate plant collector, though of a rather different stamp. Behind his surgery is a garden with paths of pebblemosaic where a plum tree casts its shadow, like a sundial, on the whitewashed walls, and there are raised beds for growing medicinal herbs. Most of the herbs he has gathered himself, from the slopes of the Snow Range: heaven's hemp (for the bladder); orchid root (for migrane); Meconopsis horridula (for dysentery); and a lichen that will cure shrunken ovaries, or bronchitis if taken with bear's grease.

He owes much of his botanical knowlegde to his student days in Nanjing. But some he learned from the strange, solitary European—with red face, spectacles and a terrible temper—who taught him his first smattering of English; at whom, as his retinue passed up the village street, the boys would clamour: 'Le-Ke! Le-Ke!' — 'Rock! Rock!' — and scamper out of reach.

Joseph F. Rock—'Dr. Lock' as the Naxi remember him—was the Austro-American botanist and explorer who lived in the Lijiang Valley, off and on from 1922 to 1949. He is our excuse for coming here. My interest in him goes back many years to a summer evening in the Arnold Arboretum in Boston, when I found that all the trees I liked best bore Rock's name on their labels.

'Tell me,' the Doctor asked on a previous visit, 'Why was Le-Ke so angry with us?'

'He wasn't angry with you,' I said. 'He was born angry.'

I should perhaps have added that the targets of his anger included the National Geographic magazine (for rewriting his prose), his Viennese nephew, Harvard University, women, the State Department, the Guomindang, Reds, red tape, missionaries, Holy Rollers, Chinese bandits and bankrupt Western civilization.

Rock was the son of an Austrian manservant who ended up as major-domo to a Polish nobleman, Court Potocki. His mother died when he was six. At 13, already under the spell of an imaginary Cathay, he taught himself Chinese characters. I like to think that, from the library of his father's employer, he read, and acted on, Count Potocki's novel of aristocrats in far-flung places: 'The Saragossa Manuscript'.

Tuberculosis not withstanding, young Rock ran away to sea: to Hamburg, to New York, to Honolulu—where, without training, he set himself up as the botanist of the Hawaiian Islands. He wrote three indispensable books on the flora, then went to Burma in search of a plant to cure leprosy. He 'discovered' Lijiang, thereafter to be the base for his travels along the Tibetan border: to the former kingdoms of Muli,

Choni and Yungning, and to the mountain of Minya Konka, which, in a moment of rashness, he claimed to be the highest in the world. (He had miscalculated by about a mile.) Yet, though he introduced hundreds of new or rare plants to Western gardens and sent off thousands and thousands of herbarium specimens, he never wrote a paper on the botany of China.

Instead, he gave his life to recording the customs, ceremonies and the unique pictographic script of his Naxi friends. Lijiang was the only home he ever knew; and after he was booted out, he could still write, in a letter, 'I want to die among those beautiful mountains rather than in a bleak hospital bed all alone.'

This, then, was the meticulous autodidact, who would pack David Copperfield in his baggage to remind him of his wretched childhood; who travelled 'en prince' (at the expense of his American backers), ate off gold plate, played records of Caruso to mountain villagers and liked to glance back, across a hillside, at his cavalcade 'half a mile long'.

His book The Ancient Nakhi Kingdom of South-West China, with its eye-aching genealogies and dazzling asides, must be one of the most eccentric publications ever produced by the Harvard University Press.

Here is a stretch of his embattled prose: 'A short distance beyond, at a tiny temple, the trail ascends the red hills covered with oaks, pines, Pinus armandi, P. yunnanensis, Alnus, Castanopsis delavayi, rhododendrons, roses, berberis, etc., up over limestone mountains, through oak forest, to a pass with a few houses called Ch'ou-shui-ching (Stinking water well). At this place many hold-ups and murders were committed by the bandit hordes of Chang Chiehpa. He strung up his victims by the thumbs to the branches of high trees, and tied rocks to their feet; lighting a fire beneath he left them to their fate. It was always a dreaded pass for caravans. At the summit there are large groves of oaks (Quercus delavayi) . . .'

No wonder Ezra Pound adored it!

Pound appears to have got hold of Rock's Nakhi Kingdom in 1956, at a time when he was locked up as a lunatic in St. Elizabeth's Hospital in Washington; from it, he extrapolated the upland paradise that was to be, in effect, his lifeline.

Over the last week we have been walking the roads of Lijiang country and finding, to our delight, that the world Rock 'saved us for memory'—to say nothing of Ezra Pound's borrowings—is very far from dead.

At Rock's former lodgings in Lijiang town, we have seen his bookcase, his pigeonhole desk, his wide chair ('because he was so fat!') and the remains of his garden beside the Jade Stream.

At Nuluko (the name means 'the foot of the silver cliffs') his country house is *almost as he left it, except that, instead of herbarium specimens, the porch is spread with drying turnip tops. The present occupant, Li Wenbiao, was one of Rock's muleteers; he showed us the master's camp bed and the washhouse where he would set up a canvas bath from Abercrombie & Fitch.*

We have been to Tiger Leaping Gorge and seen the cliff line plummeting 11,000 feet into the Yangzi. We have watched the Naxi women coming down from the Snow Range, with their bundles of pine and artemisia; and one old woman with a bamboo winnowing basket on her back, and the sun's rays passing through it:

Artemisia

Arundinaria

Winnowed in fate's tray . . . .

—'Canto CXII'

The wild pear trees are scarlet in the foothills, the larches like golden pagodas; the north slopes 'blue-green with juniper'. The last of the gentians are in flower, and flocks of black sheep brindle the plain.

When the stag drinks at the salt spring

and sheep come down with the gentian sprout . . . .

—'Canto CXII'

One evening, walking back to town across the fields, I came on a boy and girl reading aloud beside the embers of a fire. Their book was a traditional Chinese romance and, on its open page, there was a picture of Guanyin, Goddess of Mercy.

The Naxi are a passionate people, and even today, rather than submit to a hated marriage, young lovers may poison or drown themselves, or jump to their death from the mountain.

At the Naxi Institute in Lijiang, we were shown a pair of pine saplings, adorned like Christmas trees, commemorating two people who killed themselves for love. Rock wrote that such suicides become 'windspirits', reminding Pound of Dante's Paolo and Francesca, whose shades were 'so light on the wind,' and who,

readers of the Inferno will remember, fell in love while reading a romance of
chivalry.

At Shigu, where the Yangzi takes a hairpin bend, we have seen the Stone Drum:

by the waters of Stone Drum,
 the two aces . . . .
—'Canto CI'

The drum is a cylinder of marble in a pavilion by the willows. The 'aces' refers
to two Chinese generals—one lost in legend, the other of the Ming Dynasty, whose
victory is recorded on the drum itself. Our friend Tzong-Zung raised his hand to the
surface and rattled off the characters:

Snowflakes the size of a hand
Rain joining sunset to sunset
The wind quick as arrows . . . .
Commands quick as lightning
And the bandits loose their gall . . . .
Their black flag falls to the earth . . . .
They run for their lives . . . .
Heads heaped like grave mounds
Blood like rain . . . .
The dikes choked with armour and rattan shields
The trail of foxes and the trail of jackals
Have vanished from the battlefield . . . .

Rock wrote of a tradition that, should the Stone Drum split, a catastrophe will
fall on the country. About fifteen years ago, some Red Guards did, indeed, split it.
(It has since been stuck together.) We wondered if, secretly, the iconoclasts had seen
the foxes and jackals in themselves. We have listened to a Naxi orchestra that in the
bad years would practise in secret: on a stringless lute, a muffled drum and a flute
tuned at a right angle to the mouthpiece.
  In the hills above Rock's village is the Jade Summit Monastery, Yufengsi, where
we have sat with the lama hearing him tell how he would sneak into the monastery
at night, on pain of prison or worse, to save the 500-year-old camellia that

stretches, trained on a trellis, around the temple court.

Of all the places we have seen, the monastery seems the loveliest. But this is what Rock had to say of it: 'It is the home of rats, whose excrements lie inches deep . . . . dangerous to visit . . . . books wrapped in dusty silks . . . . the most forlorn and forsaken lamasery I know of.'

Also paying his respects to the lama was the Regional Commissioner for Monuments. I asked him about the horribly battered temple, dating from the Tang Dynasty, which we could see in the valley below. It is dedicated to the mountain god, Saddo, lord of the Snow Range, and protector from calamities.

The Commissioner answered, emphatically: 'The restoration will begin next month,' as if also to say that the world's oldest, subtlest, most intelligent civilization has now returned to the sources of its ancient wisdom.

In the village of Baisha, around the corner from the Doctor's house, there is another, smaller temple, its garden desolate, its cypresses fallen, its balustrades smeared with graffiti: 'Confess and we will be lenient!'

Here, under Daoist symbols of the Eternal Return, the Red Guards set up their so-called courts. Yet it occurred to us that these ill-tempered scrawls were not, after all, so distant from the spirit of the Daodejing (Tao-te-ching) of Laozi (Lao-tze):

How did the great rivers and seas gain dominion over the hundred lesser streams?
By being lower than they.

The sun goes down behind the mountain, and we must, finally, say goodbye to the Doctor. He is anxious to give me from his pharmacy a plant with the windblown name of 'Saussurea gossipiphora', which only grows on the snow line. Soon, he hopes to leave his practice in the care of his son and be free to gather herbs in the mountains. He lifts his eyes to Jade Dragon Peak and, suddenly, in his silver great-coat, becomes the living image of my favourite upland traveller, the poet Li Bo (as he appears in later pictures):

You ask me why I live in the gray hills.
I smile but do not answer, for my thoughts are elsewhere.
Like peach petals carried by the stream, they have gone
To other climates, to countries other than the world of men.

Bruce Chatwin was an eminent novelist and travel writer. His books include The Songlines, In Patagonia, On the Black Hill *and* The Viceroy of Ouidah. *This article first appeared in the* New York Times Magazine *(16 March 1986), as 'In China: Rock's Kingdom'.*

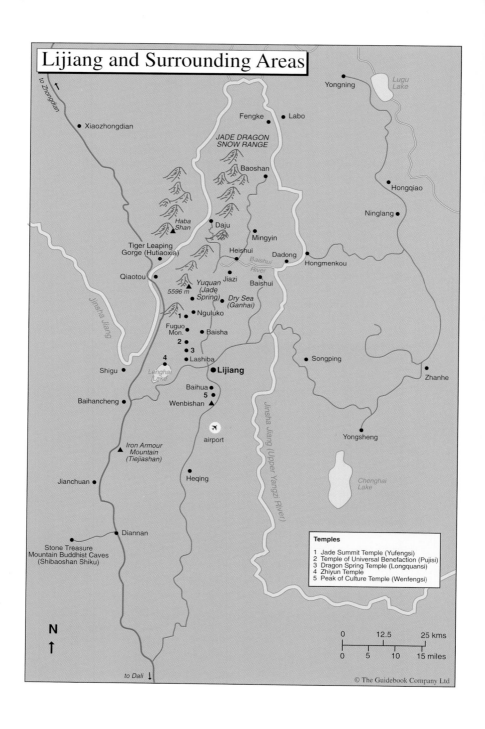

Lijiang and Surrounding Areas

to Zhongdian

Xiaozhongdian

Yongning

Lugu Lake

Fengke • Labo

JADE DRAGON
SNOW RANGE

Baoshan

Hongqiao

Ninglang •

Haba Shan ▲ Daju

Mingyin

Tiger Leaping
Gorge (Hutiaoxia)

Heishui

Dadong

Hongmenkou

Baishui River

Qiaotou

Jinsha Jiang

Jiazi

Baishui

Yuquan (Jade
Spring) •
5596 m

Dry Sea
(Ganhai) •

1

Nguluko

Fuguo
Mon. • Baisha

2

3

4 Lashiba

Shigu

Lenghai Lake

● Lijiang

Baihua

5

Wenbishan ▲

Songping

Zhanhe

Baihancheng •

airport ✈

Jinsha Jiang (Upper Yangzi River)

Yongsheng

Iron Armour
Mountain
(Tiejiashan) ▲

Jianchuan •

Heqing •

Chenghai
Lake

Diannan •

Stone Treasure
Mountain Buddhist Caves
(Shibaoshan Shiku)

Temples

1 Jade Summit Temple (Yufengsi)
2 Temple of Universal Benefaction (Pujisi)
3 Dragon Spring Temple (Longquansi)
4 Zhiyun Temple
5 Peak of Culture Temple (Wenfengsi)

N
↑

0   12.5   25 kms

0   5   10   15 miles

to Dali ↓

© The Guidebook Company Ltd

Lijiang

The remote town of Lijiang is the centre of the Naxi people, a relatively small (250,000) minority group with a richly textured culture. Lijiang, is divided by Lion Hill into two distinct parts. New Lijiang, only 35 years old, is an uninspiring, cement clone like so many modern Chinese cities while Old Lijiang is an intimate mountain town of stone and tile, laced with swift canals.

(In February 1996, Lijiang was devastated by a massive earthquake. Five counties were severely affected—Jianshan, Huangshan, Lashi, Mingyin and Baisha— leaving more than 50,000 people needing rehabilitation. While help was being administered by Chinese and international relief agencies the disaster was compounded by a series of powerful 'aftershocks' that continued to strike many months after the initial quake. A 'shock' in July 1996 left the total number of lives claimed in five months at over 300, with a further 16,000 people injured.)

Old Lijiang has been a gathering place of rugged mountain people from various ethnic groups—Lisu, Pumi, Nuosu Yi, Tibetan—but the majority are Naxi. New Lijiang, populated largely by Han Chinese, is growing and encroaching on the old city. The origin of the Naxi, like many of China's minority groups, is not fully known. Most scholars agree, however, that there was a proto-ethnic tribe, the Qiang, who dwelt in the mountains of northwestern China (today's Qinghai, Gansu and Sichuan Provinces) several thousand years ago. Northern invaders drove them south where they splintered into individual tribes. The Naxi are one of these; they speak a Tibeto-Burman language of their own.

The Naxi themselves believe they came from a common ancestor named Tabu who helped them hatch from magic eggs. Their creation myth is depicted in booklets made of resilient, insect-proof paper dating back hundreds of years. Shaman-like priests, called *dongbas*, were the only people who could read and write the unique Naxi picture-script. *Dongbas* have vanished as a functioning element in modern Naxi society, but efforts are under way to preserve their wisdom and lore.

One characteristic that strikes the visitor is the predominance of women in all types of work. Women seem to run the market and control the purse-strings. Although men are by no means indolent, they were traditionally gardeners, child-rearers and musicians. In recent years there has been a remarkable resurgence of traditional music, an ancient legacy the Naxi have kept alive since Kublai Khan's invasion in the 13th century. Twenty-two compositions remain from the original repertoire, with sweet, peaceful names such as 'Wind from the River', 'Summer has Come', 'Ten Gifts from God' and 'The Water Dragon is Singing'. At least four full orchestras of elderly men have formed in and around Lijiang. The old instruments are thrilling to see; a weathered transverse flute, a copper gong-frame, Chinese lutes, three-stringed 'banjos', enormous cymbals, a wooden fish-shaped drum. Every visitor should try to spend an evening listening to the marvellous, slow, lilting music.

Men have also always had time to indulge their passion for horses. Lijiang is still known by the nickname Land of Horses. Horses and mules are the focus of two animal fairs every April and September, reminders of grander days when Lijiang formed one end of Tibet's caravan route between India and China. The Naxi acted as middlemen, and at times a quarter of Lijiang's population was made up of Tibetan traders. The main modern road and its freight have bypassed Lijiang. Robbed of their old role, the practical Naxi now profit from their abundant forests which they harvest for timber-hungry China.

The Naxi people have had a long history of interaction with the Chinese and today, under the irresistible force of modernization, contacts are increasing and ways of life are changing fast. Nevertheless, the Naxi still desire to hold onto their cultural roots and in the remote hinterland to the north old customs continue largely untouched by the outside world.

Getting to Lijiang

Lijiang lies 196 kilometres (122 miles) north of Dali. The trip takes half a day by bus and as little as three hours by private car. Several buses leave from Xiaguan's main bus station each morning; some stop in Dali or originate from there.

Traversing the Dali Plain at sunrise, cutting through the early morning mist, with the mountains and lake all around, is a lasting experience. The road starts to climb at Upper Gate (Shangguan), the strategically important town that has always guarded Dali's northern approach. Peaceful Erhai Lake is soon out of sight. Jianchuan is the first large town along the way, 136 kilometres (85 miles) from Xiaguan. On a clear day the bright, jagged peaks of Lijiang's Jade Dragon Snow Range can be seen on the northern horizon, sharpening the traveller's anticipation. The important Buddhist cave site of Shibaoshan is southwest of Jianchuan. On the west side of the city is a small mountain called Jinhuashan. Half way up its slope the image of a Nanzhao general is carved on a cliff face, and nearby lies a sweet reclining Buddha whose rosy cheeks are created from two naturally formed red stones. Even farther west, on the banks of the Yongfeng River (Yongfenghe), stands the 18th-century Longbaota, a square, nine-tiered pagoda that rises 18 metres (59 feet). Its outstanding feature is the construction of small external shrines at each storey, with 32 Buddha images in every shrine.

Jianchuan is a county seat, predominantly Bai in its ethnic make-up. It serves as a way-station for buses. The town has a lively street market that occasionally produces remarkable items: ancient agricultural calendars; crude, handmade jewellery; and old coins.

The dividing line between the Bai and the Naxi is a high ridge called Iron

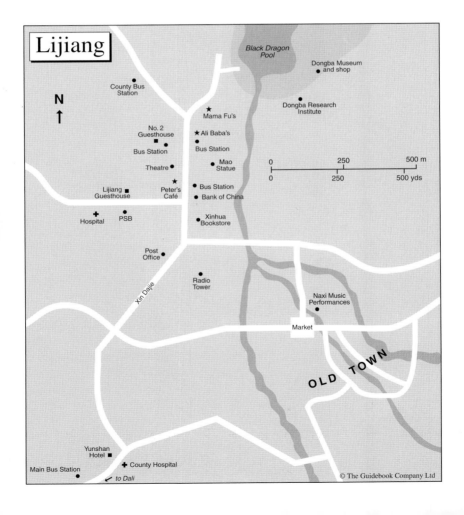

Armour Mountain (Tiejiashan). The road starts winding up it 24 kilometres (15 miles) after Jianchuan. Common lore, often borne out by observation, states that there is a preference for all things white south of Iron Armour Mountain, while to the north black is the favoured hue. For example, the Bai and Pumi minorities call themselves 'white', wear bright colours and keep white sheep and goats. Beyond the mountain, the Naxi, Tibetans, Yi, and others favour black. Women's costumes are mainly black or dark blue and domesticated animals are black. Most of their names derive from roots meaning 'black'. The point should not be stretched too far.

The main north-south road in this part of Yunnan does not go directly to Lijiang; at Baihan Chang a good paved road branches to the right. From here it is 45 kilometres (28 miles) to Lijiang, beginning with a long climb through azalea and rhododendron forests and including a wonderful straight section with an unobstructed view of the Jade Dragon Snow Range. The bus terminal is at the southwest edge of New Lijiang.

An airport has now been completed to the southeast, halfway between Lijiang and Heqing. After some teething problems regular flights began leaving in early 1996. Flights to Kunming, of which there are three a week, take just over an hour.

A final route into Lijiang for the more intrepid traveller is from Sichuan to the train junction at Panzihua (Jinjiang), followed by an eight or nine-hour drive to Lijiang. Though this is regarded as more pleasant than the Burma road be warned that this route is prone to flooding in the wet months.

Food and Drink in Lijiang

Naxi cuisine may seem indelicate; it depends on corn, wheat, beans and some rice, all of which conform to the short growing season, while the main meat is pork.

The national dish is called *baba*. There is a Naxi ditty praising the bounty of the three big local towns: Heqing for wine, Jianchuan for pretty girls, Lijiang for *baba*. *Baba* is a thick, fried wheat cake with many kinds of filling: meat, onions, jam, melted sugar, honey, pork fat. A variation is *nuomi baba*, a smallish, chewy pancake of glutinous rice stuffed with something sweet. Some *babas* are really quite good and perfect for taking on picnics.

The Naxi make good wine which they drink from childhood. Honey wine (*yinjiu*) is a smoky, nutty, honey-flavoured wine somewhat like sherry. Before the communist revolution of 1949, wine shops, run by women, abounded in towns, where men spent endless hours gossiping. Yinjiu is now bottled commercially, for local distribution, and can be bought at stalls throughout Lijiang.

(Preceding pages) *Naxi musicians, Lijiang*

Sights in the Lijiang Region

BLACK DRAGON POOL (HEILONGTAN)

At the north end of town, directly under the steep slope of Elephant Hill, is Black Dragon Pool, the best known and most frequently visited park in Lijiang. Walkways, willow and chestnut trees surround the pool, really a small lake or pond. Lijiang's picture-postcard view incorporates a willow, Black Dragon Pool, Moon-Embracing Pavilion (see below) and the towering snowy mountains as a backdrop.

The main entrance is guarded by four stone lions that originally protected the Temple of Mu Tian Wang, now destroyed. Passing through and going to the right, the first building is a library. It was brought to this site in 1982 from its original home at Fuguosi, where it was the second gate hall of that temple. Its reconstruction and repair were well handled by an old Naxi artisan. The building possesses intricately joined, beautifully painted eaves.

The second building, just beyond the library, houses the Dongba Cultural Research Institute (see below).

Further along is Dragon God Temple (Longshenci), now turned into an exhibition hall for seasonal horticultural shows and art displays. It is a 17th-century structure with nice permanent gardens of forsythia, cherry and bonsai.

The most flamboyant structure within the park is Five Phoenix Hall (Wufenglou), built in the first years of the 17th century and moved to this spot from Fuguosi between 1976 and 1979. Together with the library, Wufenglou is all that remains from the temple complex of Fuguosi, 30 kilometres (19 miles) to the west, the oldest and formerly one of the most important Tibetan monasteries of Lijiang. This wooden building received the name Five Phoenix Hall from its exaggerated eaves; there are eight flaring roof points on each of the three storeys and an observer is always supposed to see at least five of these 'phoenixes' from any angle. A museum on the first floor, dusty and haphazardly kept, is filled with exotic and artistic gems. On display are clothes, headdresses and swords of the *dongbas*, painted scrolls and dongba manuscripts, Tibetan prayer wheels and artifacts, along with charms, amulets and arcane shamanistic paraphernalia. Arrangements to see the museum should be made through the Dongba Institute.

Moon-Embracing Pavilion (Deyuelou) is the serene, beautifully proportioned structure that holds a place of honour next to Black Dragon Pool and the white marble Belt Bridge. The original three-storey pavilion dated from the late Ming Dynasty (1368–1644) and survived without significant damage until 1950. In that year, it is told with some glee, a high official took his paramour to Moon-Embracing Pavilion, where together they ate cakes and drank wine until the moon rose. Then

The Age-old 'rammed earth' method of building walls in northwestern Yunnan. Workers use heavy, specially designed poles to pound earth between a frame of fixed boards. The earth rises higher and higher until finally the boards are removed to reveal the finished wall.

the couple spread oil about, ignited it and offered themselves up in a spectacular double suicide, destroying the pavilion in the process. The present pavilion is a reconstruction from 1962. Belt Bridge, so named because it resembles a mandarin official's belt, was also rebuilt after 1949.

DONGBA CULTURAL RESEARCH INSTITUTE (DONGBA WENHUA YANJIUSHI)

Following the Chinese revolution of 1949, the folklore and history of the Naxi people might have been lost were it not for a few local scholars who started a small museum in 1954. The Yunnan Academy of Social Sciences incorporated it into a formal institute in 1981, the Dongba Cultural Research Institute. Its purpose is to study, document and preserve the ancient Naxi culture of the *dongbas,* religious shamans who played a pivotal role in traditional society. Only 30 or so dongbas are still alive, and a handful of these men are attached to the institute. Researchers are primarily engaged in the laborious work of translating thousands of *dongbajing* into Chinese. These small 'booklets', written in an archaic and peculiar script, are read aloud and taken down syllable by syllable; Naxi meaning and grammar are unscrambled and put into Chinese form and finally a proper translation is made. Awaiting scholars are the deeper investigations into the intriguing fields of *dongba* religion, mythology, origination and history.

About a thousand of these booklets were written over the centuries, covering subjects ranging from accounting, through history and mythology, to exorcism and magic. Some 20,000 copies are scattered around the world. The Dongba Institute has approximately 5,000; the rest are in foreign university collections and a few in private hands. The goal of the Institute is to preserve, record, and ultimately produce an encyclopaedia of Naxi culture.

FIVE MAIN TEMPLES OF LIJIANG (LIJIANG WUDA MINGSI)

The 17th century was a great period of economic, political and cultural flowering in Lijiang. This renaissance is embodied in the life and works of Celestial King Mu, Mu Tian Wang, ruler from the ancient lineage of Naxi chiefs. Mu Tian Wang came to power in 1598 at the age of 11 and within two decades had chalked up a string of accomplishments that would be added to as his reign continued: poet and author, and an exemplary administrator who supervised large public works and enriched the entire region, he was appointed guardian of China's frontiers and pacified rebels and brigand tribes. The Ming Empire lavished deeds and titles upon him, built arches and town gates in his honour, and held up this non-Chinese as a model for other border peoples to emulate.

For all these worldly achievements, Mu Tian Wang was a deeply religious man who championed Buddhism through printing and publishing Buddhist works and through the support of communities of monks. He had a direct hand in the construction of major temples around Lijiang and paid for the establishment of an important monastery on Chicken Foot Mountain (Jizushan) in the area east of Dali.

His contributions were for the propagation of the Karmapa school of Tibetan Buddhism. The practices of this school, dating from the mid-12th century, have always been closely bound up with the life of the common people, aiming not so much at theoretical knowledge as at its practical realization. Yoga and magic were frequently employed in Lijiang, on the wild border of Tibet, mixing with, and borrowing from, the dongba religion.

The main temples described below, patronized by Mu Tian Wang in the 17th century, are (or rather, were) all embodiments of the Karmapa school.

Jade Summit Temple (Yufengsi) lies 11 kilometres (7 miles) northwest of Lijiang high up on a mountainside in the midst of pine woods, commanding a magnificent view over the valley. The group of buildings with white and grey tiled roofs is connected by stone steps and paths on several terraced levels. The first large hall on the left is the main Buddha hall, now acting as a friendly teahouse. It has remnants of Tibetan-style murals. To the right is a small cluster of enclosed buildings with a shrine containing a strange assortment of faded pictures. Yufengsi's sole monk resides here, shuffling around and happy to dress up in his old ecclesiastical robe at the mention of a photograph.

The one superior building, at the highest level of the temple complex, deserves slow savouring. Its courtyard is laid out in beautiful geometric pebbled designs, doors and windows are finely carved, and in the middle, close to the entrance, grows a remarkable centrepiece, an enormous and ancient camellia tree famous throughout Yunnan. Each year in late February or early March it unfailingly opens to display '20,000 blossoms'. Whether this number is actually correct becomes insignificant in the face of such a *tour de force* of nature. Everyone far and wide cherishes this tree so it is essential to avoid Yufengsi on overcrowded Sundays.

Temple of Universal Benefaction (Pujisi) sits above the village of Pujicun, 5 kilometres (3 miles) northwest of Lijiang. From the plain it takes half an hour to climb through a maze of steep goat trails to reach the temple. Don't give up; local herdsmen will point you in the right direction. Two huge trees, Chinese flowering crab apple (*haitang*), stand within the courtyard. Beyond them is the Buddha hall, formerly desecrated, but still containing murals, Buddha images and thankas, Tibetan

A woman of the Naxi minority

painted scroll-banners presenting pictorial instruction on theology, astrology, and the lives of Buddhas, saints and deities. There are ruins above Pujisi that offer a fine view over the green and yellow fields far, far below.

Peak of Culture Temple (Wenfengsi) lies under the unmistakable landmark of Calligraphic Brush Mountain (Wenbishan) 9 kilometres (5.5 miles) south of Lijiang. The mountain, steep and pointed, is the most conspicuous within the Huangshan Range. The road to Wenfengsi passes through Baihua, the richest village in the entire region. At the foot of the mountain it begins a long climb along a rugged dirt track. It is much nicer to leave the vehicle here and walk straight up to the temple through orchards and woods, silent save for the birds. This once-famous complex was ruined in the 1960s, then rebuilt, and is now looked after by two old monks. It is still a marvellous and holy place, hidden within a glade surrounded by giant, shady trees. There remain some gems of painting and carving: Tibetan mandalas and writing, the Eight Sacred Emblems of Buddhism, roof murals (still bright and beautiful) and six central square red columns with lotiform capitals.

Wenfengsi was a centre for occult and ascetic practices. Just above the temple at the edge of the forest is a sacred spring where initiates underwent an amazing training. A simple hole in the earth nearby became the home of an ascetic who would proceed to spend three years, three months and three days within, meditating, chanting, praying and doing battle with psychic demons. Local monks would think nothing of striking out on foot for a two- or three-year walk to the great pilgrimage sites of Tibet.

If you want a good hike, it is a three-hour walk from the temple to the top of holy Wenbishan.

Zhiyunsi, the fourth main temple, has been converted into a school for the children of Lashiba, a town southwest of Lijiang. Nothing remains of **Fuguosi** (Kingdom of Blessing Temple), oldest of the five temples, except for one small house. Two important buildings were transported intact from the original site to Black Dragon Pool Park in Lijiang.

DRAGON SPRING TEMPLE (LONGQUANSI)

This minor temple lies west of Lijiang near the village of Wenmingcun at the base of low pine-covered hills. Longquansi is thoroughly dilapidated but has a kind of random beauty about it. A compact and cosy courtyard is filled with primula, orchids, peach trees, citrus and roses. The god at the main table altar is in the *dongba* style and the nearby Chinese characters mean 'happiness for every family'. The murals are all ruined but some excellent wood carving remains on doors, windows and railings, with motifs from Daoism, Buddhism and animism.

BAISHA VILLAGE AND GREAT PRECIOUS STOREHOUSE TEMPLE (DABAOJI GONG)

Baisha is the most important village on the plain north of Lijiang. It was the Naxi capital before Kublai Khan came south to claim this region as part of the Yuan Empire (1279–1368), at which time Lijiang was made the centre. The name Baisha is the sinicized form of Boashi, which means 'dead Pumi', a reference to the victorious battle and slaughter of the Pumi tribe in ancient times.

Great Precious Storehouse Temple (Dabaoji Gong) is also known as Coloured Glaze Temple (Liulidian). It can be found near the village school, which is itself a converted temple. The complex was built and decorated over a period of more than 200 years, from 1385 to 1619, employing the eclectic artistic energies of Chinese Daoists, Tibetan and Naxi Buddhists and local dongba shamans. This rich fusion has resulted in a tremendously powerful art, heavy in spirit and awe-inspiring in its presentation of the mystical world. Dominated by black, silver, dark green, gold and red colours, the murals in the back hall, overlaid with centuries of brown soot, are doom-laden and bizarre. The scenes and figures, some still vivid in detail, are largely taken from Tibetan Buddhist iconography and include the Wheel of

A Muslim man near the Stone Forest

Life, judges of the underworld, the damned, titans and gods, Buddhas and bodhisattvas. There are trigrams, lotus flowers and even Sanskrit inscriptions on the ceiling. The deliberate damage done to the paintings is apparent and terrible, but the loss of the irreplaceable wooden statuary that filled the temple, of which there is no trace, is even more tragic.

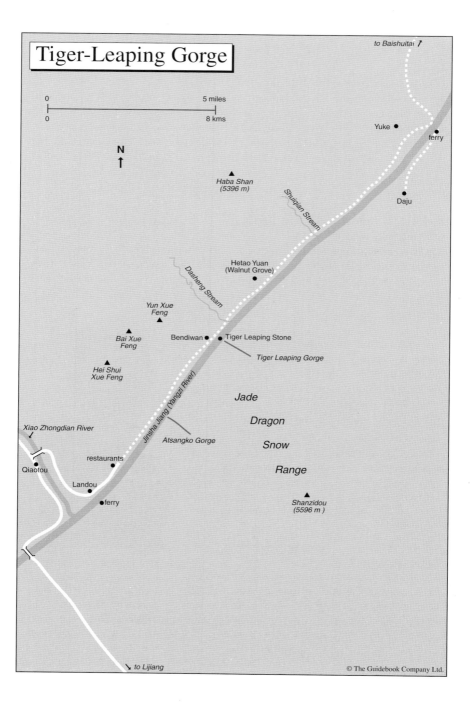

Tiger-Leaping Gorge

to Baishuitai ↗

0 | 5 miles
0 | 8 kms

N
↑

Yuke ●

● ferry

▲ Haba Shan
(5396 m)

Daju ●

Shuiqian Stream

Hetao Yuan
(Walnut Grove) ●

Dasheng Stream

Yun Xue
Feng
▲

Bendiwan ● ● Tiger Leaping Stone

▲ Bai Xue
Feng

Tiger Leaping Gorge

▲ Hei Shui
Xue Feng

Jade

Jinsha Jiang (Yangzi River)

Dragon

Snow

Xiao Zhongdian River

Range

Atsangko Gorge

restaurants ●

Qiaotou ●

Landou ●

▲ Shanzidou
(5596 m)

● ferry

↘ to Lijiang

© The Guidebook Company Ltd.

A separate building called Pavilion of Great Calm (Dadingge) stands outside the front wall of the main temple. Although built later, in the Qing Dynasty (1644-1911), it is considered part of the whole grouping, and though damaged has some exquisite, delicate paintings of flowers, birds and jewellery.

JADE DRAGON SNOW RANGE (YULONGXUESHAN)

The formidable Jade Dragon Mountains dominate the Lijiang Plain, defining its western edge with their towering mass. The mountains' western flanks drop steeply to the Upper Yangzi River (Jinsha Jiang), helping to form magnificent, deep gorges, and the highest peak is Shanzidou, at 5,596 metres (18,360 feet). Storms frequently rage around the glaciers, rocks and perpetual snowfields of the five primary summits. However, the alpine meadows on the lower slopes, where herders sing to their goats and cattle and collectors of wild medicinal herbs go happily about their business, are excellent hiking country. Such excursions are a natural extension of visits to the many temple sites around Lijiang.

NGULUKO, THE HOME OF JOSEPH ROCK

Nguluko (Chinese: Xuesongcun, Snow Pine Village) is a small, typical Naxi village, whose lovely name in the local language means 'at the foot of the silver stone mountain'. It lies slightly north of Jade Lake Village (Yuhucun) and is unremarkable except for being touched by a remarkable man.

In 1922 an Austro-American botanist and explorer named Joseph Rock arrived in Lijiang and made this area his home on and off for the next 29 years. He was a contrary man of tremendous energy and terrible temper who lived like a foreign prince in the wilds of western China, always engaged in activities from plant collecting and surveying to photography and linguistics. His prodigious output of articles and books and contributions to several sciences is impressive. He will probably be best remembered for the introduction of innumerable plant species to the West and his rigorous works on Naxi ethnology.

Nguluko, Rock's country home, was where he kept his retinue of a dozen Naxi servants perpetually busy, pressing plants for herbaria, summing up the discoveries and specimens of the last expedition or preparing for the next one. His house still stands, and is today owned by the family of Li Wenbiao, Rock's own muleteer. Here is the site of the accomplishments of a strange and splendid man. The house is a good example of Naxi domestic architecture; a wall and gateway that open onto a three-sided courtyard, the residence ahead, and the wood and animal shelters aside.

Markets and Wineshops

*S*tarting in distant villages early in the morning, the streams of farmers began to emerge on Likiang soon after ten o'clock, along five main roads. The streets were jammed with horses loaded with firewood; people bringing charcoal in baskets on their backs and others carrying vegetables, eggs and poultry. Pigs were either carried, tied up, on poles by two men, or led by women, who held the leash in one hand and gently prodded the the animal with a switch in the other. Many other kinds of merchandise were carried either on the backs of the people themselves or on their animals. There was the noise of hooves on hard stone, loud talk, shouting and much laughter. In the market itself there was great tumult with all these crowds trying to pass each other and jockeying for the best positions on the square. On the previous night sturdy stalls had already been pulled out of the common pile, or dragged from surrounding shops and set in rows in the centre. Women and girls brought heavy bales of textiles and spread bolts of cloth on the stalls. Haberdashery, spices and vegetables were displayed in separate rows. Shortly after noon the market was in full swing and was a boiling cauldron of humanity and animals. At about three o'clock the market session reached its climax and then began to decline.

Main street was lined with dozens of 'exclusive bars' and thither thirsty villagers, men and women, turned their steps. After a tiring day in the market the numerous tea-shops in Chinese towns and villages are crowded with congenial parties of men and women relaxing over pots of tea. In this respect, the customs of Likiang were quite distinct. There were no tea-shops, and if anyone drank tea at all during the day it was brewed in miniature earthen jugs on the brazier concealed somewhere in the back room. Everyone, men, women and children, drank wine, white or sweet yintsieu. No self-respecting child above two years would go to sleep without a cup of yintsieu.

The 'exclusive bars' were neither bars nor were they exclusive. They were general stores where, in addition to salt, sugar, salted vegetables and haberdashery, wine was kept for sale, both to be taken away in customer's own jars or to be consumed on the premises. The shops were uniformly small in Likiang and, in addition to the counter facing the street, there was a longer counter at a right angle to it, leaving a narrow passage from the door ro the inner rooms of the shop. A couple of narrow benches were put before this counter and there the people sat drinking wine.

Anyone could have a drink at any shop, but some villagers acquired preferences for particular shops. These regular and faithful customers grew intimate with the lady owner, and always gave her the first option on whatever they were bringing to the market for sale. Similarly the lady favoured them with special discounts on whatever they wanted to buy from her. Actually such relations between the established clients and the shop owner were not so simple. The lady also acted as their broker, banker, postmaster and confidante. Baskets with purchases were left in her keeping whilst the customers went out for more shopping. Small loans were negotiated with her on the security of the next deliveries of whatever they usually brought to the market or against growing chickens or pigs. When clients could not pay for their drinks or purchase, credit transactions were permitted by the lady, who got her husband or son to record them in simple Chinese. Wallets with cash were sometimes deposited at the shop for safe-keeping by the farmers whose villages were not safe from robbers. As their was no postal service to remote villages, the wine-shop was a favourite accommodation address. Letters were duly forwarded to the recipients by safe hands. Confidential advice was sought by the clients from the lady on the problems of engagement and marriage, childbirth and funerals. And, of course, every lady wine-shop owner was a Bureau of Information par excellence. She knew the curricula vitae of everybody within a radius of a hundred miles, and I doubt whether there ever existed a secret in Likiang that was not known to her.

Madame Lee was an old woman, very erect, stately and handsome, with aquiline features and large lustrous eyes. She belonged to the cream of Likiang society and was much respected both in the town and in the villages. Everybody knew her and she knew everybody.

It was not easy to get a seat at Madame Lee's shop in the late afternoon. In an emergency she permitted me to sit behind the counter on a small stool, facing the other customers. Men and women came to have a drink or two before starting on their trek back to the village: but in accordance with nakhi customs, no woman sat down in company with a man. Women usually took their drinks standing in front of the shop and chatting meanwhile with Madame Lee. It was quite common for women to treat men to drinks; nobody tried to prevent her from paying the bill. As soon as his drink was finished, a man would go and somebody else would drop into his place. It was wonderful to sit at the back of the shop in comparative gloom, and watch through the wide window the movement in the narrow street, as though seeing on a screen a colour film of surpassing beauty. Sooner or later everybody who had attended the market session had to pass through Main Street at least once or twice. Old friends could be seen and invited for a drink or new acquaintances made. Any stranger could be waved to and asked to share a pot of wine, without any ceremony or introduction, and I was sometimes stopped in street by total strangers and offered a cigarette or a drink. No such liberties were allowed for women, but now and then one of them, who knew me well, would slap me on the shoulder and say, 'Come and let us have a drink!' and she would have to take her drink standing up so as to avoid a local scandal.

With the deep blue sky and brilliant sunshine, the street was a blaze of colour, and as we sat and sipped our wine from Madame Lee's porce lain cups, mountain youths, in the sheer joy of life, would dance through the streets playing flutes like the pipes of Pan. They looked wild woodland creatures in their sleeveless jerkins and short skin pants.

Occasionally something would happen to shock or amuse the town. Once, I remember, a stark-naked man appeared in the market and proceeded leisurely up Main Street. I was sitting at Madame Lee's. He went from shop to shop, asking for a drink or a cigarette. Women spat and turned away their faces but nothing was done to stop him. The truth was that the brazen Likiang women could hardly be shocked by anything, but they had to put on some show of modesty and embarrassment in order to avoid acid and biting gibes from the men. A policeman was never to be seen in the streets, and it was only at the end of the day, when somebody bothered to rout one out from the police station, that the demented man was led away. He was not jailed, for there were no laws or statutes in Likiang about indecency in public. Such matters were largely decided by public opinion. One could always go a few hundred yards towards the park and see dozens of naked Tibetans and Nakhi swimming in the river or lying on the grass in the sun in full view of the passers-by and in front of the houses.There was a lot of giggling and whispering amongst the passing women and girls, but there were no complaints. A line, however, had to be drawn against nakedness in the public market.

Peter Goullart, Forgotten Kingdom, 1957

Inscribed Stone at Jade Lake Village (Yuhucun)

A historically important monument stands at the back of Jade Lake Village near the base of the mountains, 15 kilometres (9.5 miles) northwest of Lijiang. It is an 18-metre (59-foot) high limestone wall inscribed with the two epigraphs 'a jade pillar supports Heaven' and 'jade wall and golden river', the latter a reference to the Jade Dragon Mountains and the Golden Sands River Jinsha Jiang, common name for the Upper Yangzi). A Qing-Dynasty official, representative of the emperor, completed the inscription in 1724, thus imprinting the fateful year that marked full Chinese control over Naxi political life.

Traditional headdress of a Hani woman

Dry Sea (Ganhai)

The Dry Sea is a section of the Lijiang plain 22 kilometres (14 miles) north of the city that receives less rain than other areas. The road runs straight through the middle of the valley, parallel to the mountains on the left. This is the road to Daju. Agriculture is replaced by the rock-strewn plain of Amendu, a curious name meaning 'Rocks Without Tails'. The road rises slowly but steadily until it crosses a gentle pass and breaks up into random tracks that crisscross one another in a dry 'sea' of short brown grass, sand and stones. Occasional lone pines break the monotony as the road skirts the base of the mountains, giving an exceptionally close view of the Jade Dragon massif.

Black Water, White Water (Heibaishui)

The road picks up again at the far edge of the Dry Sea and climbs into the mountains past vistas of long, forested valleys with no sign of human habitation. Water is finally reached after several kilometres at the swift river of White Water (Baishui), named for the white stones in the riverbed. The limestone, washed down from mountain peaks, sometimes contains recognizable coral, proof that this land once lay deep below the ocean. Further up the mountain rushes Black Water (Heishui) in a bed of black rock. Tradition dictates that you drink only the white water.

Roads and logging camps in the area have changed traditional patterns of tribal interaction and now Naxi meet and mingle with the indigenous Yi, who, with 30 branches and distribution over four provinces, are China's fourth largest minority.

Heishui is also a small Yi community high in the hills north of Lijiang, with a population of perhaps 250 people. The village is close to the pine forests that rise steeply up the Jade Dragon slopes, and the immediate area is composed of cleared fields for potatoes, corn, and the small flocks and herds of the locals. Terracing and fences protect the fields and plots from erosion and animals.

Women as well as men wear the black felt cloak. They live in the most primitive fashion; their houses made of pine boards, tied together with vines, are not much better than pigsties ... When not occupied cultivating their land, they hold up lonely travellers and rob their Naxi and Chinese neighbours.

Joseph Rock, 1935

The roughcut timber, planks and clothing can still be found here, though influence from the 'big city' of Lijiang is evident. Smoky fires still form the center of family life. Heishui is a good point of departure for high pastures, forests and ridges of the mountains.

Tiger leaping gorge

BEYOND HEIBAISHUI

Downstream from the confluence of Heibaishui lies the small community of Jiazi, and further still downstream the fascinating town of Dadong, a traditional Naxi community. Twenty kilometres (13 miles) to the northeast of Dadong on the Yangzi lies Hongmenkou, the site where Kublai Khan's army made the treacherous river crossing on inflated skin boats in the 13th century to conquer the Dali Kingdom. Farther north still is the ancient walled town of Baoshan Gu Shi Cheng (Baoshan Ancient Stone City), one of the last of its kind in China.

BAOSHAN STONE CITY

Nearly 130 kilometres northeast of Lijiang lies the remarkable community of Baoshan Shi Gu Cheng (Baoshan Ancient Stone City), usually called Baoshan, but not to be confused with the much larger Baoshan, the main city of western Yunnan, southwest of Dali. This Baoshan has only 100 families. It occupies a dazzling site, high on a ridge overlooking the Upper Yangzi River (Jin Sha Jiang), surrounded by tightly ascending terraced fields. Many of the houses are carved from the living rock or have sections made from the red stone. Some even have tables, stools, beds and cupboards cut from the rocky ridge.

DAJU XIAN

Daju is a collection of isolated Naxi villages on a large plain near the north entrance to Tiger Leaping Gorge, on the Upper Yangzi beneath the Jade Dragon Snow Range. It is a region of stark beauty amidst nature's hugeness. Haba, second tallest mountain of the range and only one on the far side of the Yangzi, is across the water where the Tibetan counties of Yunnan begin. Daju is famous and necessary for the ferry crossing that leads to the Tiger Leaping Gorge trail.

TIGER LEAPING GORGE (HUTIAOXIA)

After the renowned Three Gorges (Sanxia) in Sichuan and Hubei, Hutiaoxia is the Yangzi's best known gorge. Wedged tightly between titanic cliffs, the river is so narrow here, so legend tells us, that a hunted tiger made his escape to the other side in a single bound. Yunnan's main northern road to Tibet crosses the Yangzi near the gorge at Lunan, 90 kilometres (56 miles) from Lijiang. From Qiaotou it is possible to see how such a geological phenomenon was created: two huge mountains leaning close to each other and a large volume of fast moving water between them cutting deeper and deeper into the bottom of the gorge. In some places there is a drop of 3,000 metres (10,000 feet) to the water, a beautiful and vertiginous place to go for a walk (map page 134).

STONE DRUM (SHIGU)

The village of Stone Drum stands at the First Great Bend of the Yangzi River, 70 kilometres (44 miles) west of Lijiang. The route from Lijiang follows the main road to Dali for 45 kilometres (28 miles), then branches west by a good, unpaved road that winds downward towards the river through huge forests.

The approach to Stone Drum offers a dramatic view of the Yangzi's near-180-degree turn, where the wide, swift waters perform a miraculous about-face. For nearly 20 kilometres (12.5 miles) the river, first flowing south, then north, runs parallel to itself. Locals say if it were not for their village standing guard at the bend,

China would lose the water of the Yangzi to Southeast Asia, like that of the adjacent Mekong and Salween Rivers.

Stone Drum gets its name from a large, cylindrical, marble tablet shaped like a drum, an engraved memorial that honours the Sino-Naxi victory over a Tibetan army in the summer of 1548. It was an awful slaughter on the banks of the river. A Tibetan force of 200,000 men was completely routed and dispersed in confusion, and in gory celebration the champions decapitated nearly 3,000 of the enemy. The stone drum recounts it all: ' ... heads heaped like grave mounds, blood like rain ...'

Another military event occurred here in recent times, a small but important chapter in the story of the Long March, Chinese communism's greatest ordeal. After breaking out of the Nationalist encirclement in eastern China at the end of 1934, the Red Army of 100,000 fled westward, embarking on an epic 6,000-kilometre (3,750-mile) march through some of the country's most bitter, rugged land before finding a haven in Shaanxi Province. The main body of the army crossed the Yangzi several hundred kilometres east of Stone Drum, but 18,000 men crossed at this point. The citizenry rose to the occasion, ceaselessly ferrying troops to the northern bank in their boats, 40–60 men per trip. The entire crossing took four days and nights (24–28 April 1936) and is still remembered as the greatest event in the lives of the local Naxi. The prominent marble 'Chinese Workers and Peasants Red Army Second Route Army Long March Ferry Crossing Memorial' stands on a high promontory with a fine view over the historic site.

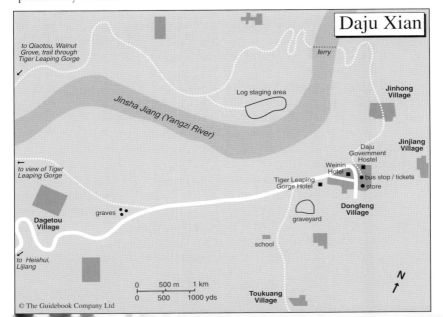

Yongning

Yongning and Lugu Lake

Northeast of Lijiang lies a gem of a lake, Lugu Hu. Though only 110 kilometres away as the crow flies, the road is much longer and takes most of a day if travelling by bus. The lake straddles the Yunnan-Sichuan border, is approximately eight kilometres across and is dotted with five small islands, three of which are considered sacred and visited regularly for sacrificial purposes. The setting is stunning. Steep hills rise along two sides of the lake, which lies at 2,685 metres above sea level, highest in the province and second deepest (90 metres) in China, the deepest being Fuxian Hu.

On the lake's Sichuan side, to the north and east, one finds a Babel where the children routinely speak three or four tongues—Moso, Tibetan, Mandarin Chinese and Pumi (Xifan). This region was historically an enclave of Bon, the archaic, pre-Buddhist religion of Tibet that relied heavily on magic and spells over nature. It is still possible to see peculiar towers, up to six metres tall, on the hills outside the main town of Zuosuo. At the top of a 'mast' sits a wooden offering tablet painted with a divinity and below a jumble of wire, twine and yarn, looking like a damaged spider web. This type of tower is called *nya-ta*, a demon trap to disarm evil forces and protect the crops below. It is also intended to prevent damaging hail. The Yunnan side of Lugu Hu is dominated by the Moso people, considered by some to be relatives of the Naxi. The Moso consider themselves to be a separate group. The Naxi call the Moso *Luxi*.

The Plain of Yongning (2,900 metres) lies 20 kilometres west of the lake and is the cultural and agricultural centre of the Moso. Yongning town is unprepossessing, with a single main street, though the surroundings are memorable. To the east rises Lion Mountain (Shizi Shan), dominant presence on the plain. To the north stand the purple ranges of Sichuan and all round the verdant fields are crisscrossed with water channels.

In the year 1253, the Mongol Kublai Khan massed his forces here before the decisive battle against the Dali Kingdom. He marched his men southward through red mountains, visible today from the hill known as *La-ba-der*. Local legend says the Great Khan himself climbed this hill to review his troops.

In former times the Yongning Monastery (Yongning Lama Si) was the most important building on the plain. It suffered badly during the Cultural Revolution, but was reconstructed with considerable care in 1990. A small chapel to the right of the main temple escaped damage and dates from the monastery's founding in the 17th century. The entire complex was and remains a Gelugpa (Yellow Hat) institution of Tibetan Buddhism.

LUGU HU (LUGU LAKE)

Lugu Hu, a beautiful body of water that straddles the Yunnan-Sichuan border, is home to a number of different minority peoples—Moso, Tibetan, Pumi, Yi and others.

From Lijiang to Lugu Lake is just over 280 kilometres by road. The route passes through Ninglang Yi Autonomous County and a large town of the same name, a fas-

Traditional tiled rooftops of Old Lijiang

cinating place to meet some of the Yi people and learn of their mountain life. Invitations to visit upland villages are sometimes given.

The main town on the Yunnan side is Yongning, 30 kilometres west of the lake. This is the home of the Moso, a group long considered a branch of the Naxi, who call these people 'Luxi'. Historically, the Moso called themselves Hlikhin and are known, somewhat sensationally throughout Yunnan, as a 'the matriarchal tribe'.

Han Chinese find Yongning and Lugu Hu an inriguing area, based on the perpetuation of myths and tales about this matriarchal system. Prurience plays a part, too. The Moso practice a custom known as *A'zhu*, whereby marriage is not announced formally, but rather a loose arrangement of cohabitation goes on for some time with various lovers. Children stay with the mother, as do the powers of decision making and control of money. Often children do not know the identity of their fathers.

Yongning is not much more than a big village with one main street. The primary sight is Yongning Monastery, a Yellow Hat centre that was reconstructed between 1889 and 1891. One small chapel, to the right of the main entrance, survived the damage of the 1950s.

It was here on the plain of Yongning that Kublai Khan massed his forces before the decisive, and victorious, battle against the Dali Kingdom in the year 1253. He camped at a place called Ri Yue He, 'union of sun and moon', beneath the hill of *La-ba-der*. It is possible to climb this steep hill southwest of town to view the famous meadow below, now a field of corn, rice and tobacco.

To the east, dominating the Yongning plain, is Lion Mountain (Shizi Shan); the rocky mass raises its head above Lugu Lake as though a living presence. In the lake are a number of islands that once were retreats of Yongning's nobility. A mountain festival and a lake festival are the two main annual events for the Moso people. The former takes place on the 25th day of the 7th lunar month (usually in August or early September), the latter on the 15th day of the 3rd lunar month (usually late April).

In the lake region, especially around Zuosuo on the Sichuan side, the pre-Buddhist Bon religion of Tibet still survives despite decades of supression. One can find on hillsides a bizarre structure, a complicated tower with a central axis or mast, embellished with an amazing array of objects. The top of the tower, six metres above the ground, holds a wooden offering tablet painted with a divinity surrounded by a green halo. Below is a rampage of twine, wire and yarn, both scrambled and coherent, like a damaged spiderweb. Amid the jumble one might find many tablets and cloth ties of varied colours. The entire tower is a *nya-ta*, a demon trap to catch and disarm evil forces. Overlooking fields and crops, it is also meant to prevent devastating hail. Bonpo monasteries survive as well; one fine wooden temple with murals stands at Zuosuo.

Tibetan Counties of Yunnan

Zhongdian

Zhongdian is the name of both a huge county and the town that is its capital. It forms one of three counties that make up the Diqing Tibetan Autonomous Prefecture in northwesternmost Yunnan; Tibetans call their home Gyelthang, not Zhongdian, an introduced Chinese name. The prefecture touches Tibet in the northwest, Ganzi and Muli in Sichuan to the north, Lijiang to the south and Nu Jiang (Salween River) Lisu Autonomous Prefecture to the west. It has a population of more than 300,000 and is at the heart of the Hengduan Mountain Range that embraces the gorge system of great rivers which rush down from Tibet. The region has a huge range in elevation, from a 6740-metre mountain on the border with Tibet to 1480 metres in river valleys to the south. Plant hunters and naturalist during the first half of this century prized the area. Now many of the forests have been stripped, but still large tracts of virgin forest remain. Domesticated animals of the region include yak, *dzo,* sheep, goats, pigs and chickens; wild animals are the Dian golden haired monkey, wild donkey, black-necked crane, lesser panda, leopard, muskdeer, pangolin, and many small mammals and birds. Hunting is universally loved here and guns are common; most of these rare treasures will not survive.

Wheat, corn, barley and potatoes are the common staples; huge ricks for drying are a common sight in the harvest season. Mushrooms are prized, for local consumption and for export, and the collection of herbs, roots and plant products for medicine play an important part in the local economy. Minerals—gold, silver, copper, iron, lead, zinc— and timber are major reasons for China's interest in this region.

The town of Zhongdian opened to tourism in 1992 and is slowly finding its place on the travellers' map. Local entrepreneurs are opening hotels, restaurants and starting tours, even encouraging foreign investment. Zhongdian is a long way from anywhere, but it should be considered seriously for a visit by anyone who is in northwest Yunnan.

The bus trip from Dali takes ten hours and from Lijiang six hours (Lijiang to Zhongdian is 200 kilometres). After Qiaotou and the entrance to Tiger Leaping Gorge, the road climbs steadily along the Xiao Zhongdian He (Small Zhongdian River), up and up through large forests that occasionaly give way to stunning vistas of distant mountain valleys and isolated hamlets. Suddenly the bus goes over a rise and one is miraculously transported onto the Tibetan Plateau, over 3000 metres in altitude, where expanses of grass and grazing yaks appear. The transition from the hot Yangzi River valley to the Tibetan highlands is as dramatic a way to approach Tibet as can be found.

Soon after arriving on the plateau, a huge white stupa comes into view on the right. This marks the site where the previous Panchen Lama gave a speech and greeted the locals in the mid-1980s. Fine domestic architecture, fields of colour and rarified air give the run into Zhongdian a magical quality.

The town itself (altitude: 3160 metres) is unprepossessing at first sight. A single, very long main street holds all the major shops and offices. Most people here are Tibetans, though Chinese magistrates and lesser officials have been in Zhongdian since the 18th century.

Most visitors stay in one of the two hotels in the southern part of town, not at the official government guesthouse. The Yung Sheng Hotel is headed by a remarkable entrepreneur named Mr He who has expanded into many economic markets. He has exported mushrooms to Japan and Europe for years.

Old Zhongdian, still entirely in local Tibetan style, is also to the south of the main street. A park on a hill here gives a view over the entire town.

'Jing Po' Festival village dance

SONGZHANLING MONASTERY

This large Yellow Hat (Gelugpa) Tibetan monastery has returned from the ashes and destruction that swept southeastern Tibet in the late 1950s and 1960s. Songsenlin was founded in the 17th century during the reign of the Great Fifth Dalai Lama, when the Yellow Hat school came to full ascendancy in Tibet. It lies a few kilometres beyond the north end of town and welcomes visitors who behave respectfully.

The monastery once had as many as 1200 monks before, and now claims many hundreds, though most of these stay at home and work with their families, only coming together as a single body on rare festival occasions. In 1980 the second delegation sent by the Dalai Lama to investigate conditions in Tibet stayed in Zhongdian, and since then there has been steady reconstruction at this sacred site.

Also at the north end of Zhongdian, to the left of the main road that continues to Benzilan, is the Zhongdian Wooden Bowl Factory (Muwan Chagn). This site churns out thousands of small wooden tea bowls, favoured by Tibetans, as well as larger bowls and special lidded containers used in households to hold sweets, popped rice, seeds or other snacks to offer guests.

Zhongdian area has a number of Buddhist sites. Red Hat Nyingma centre outside to the east, and a wonderful, secluded monastery in a bower. This second site is a few kilometres to the right of the road that leads southeast to Baidi (Sanba) and the limestone sinter terraces of Baishuitai. The drive from Zhongdian to Baidi takes three hours through impressive mountain scenery.

BAISHUITAI (WHITE WATER TERRACE)

In southeast Zhongdian County, across the Upper Yangzi from Daju and two-days' walk from Tiger Leaping Gorge, is the area known variously as Bada, Baidi or Berder (Naxi). It encompasses a broad valley that runs down steeply to join the great river 20 kilometres away.

At the head of the valley are a series of stepped terraces, white and encrusted, each with a small pool of shallow water. Such terraces can be found in other parts of the world, such as Turkey and New Zealand, but the ones here are particularly beautiful because of the dramatic setting. The water source that creates the terraces is on a flat field above; it is considered a holy spring and is honoured by the local Nakhi people with painted wooden stakes implanted around its edge. The flow of water, and consequently the extent of the terraces, is at its greatest in March, when thousands of pilgrims and tourists come to picnic and drink the water. It is believed to have curative powers and to help women conceive.

DONGBA GU DONG (ANCIENT CAVE)

At the head of the valley, across from Baishuitai, is a wooded mountain. Two-thirds of the way up its steep slope is a double-cave, two chambers that in the distant past constituted the home of Shenrap, a semi-mythical spiritual hero who Tibetans claim as the founder of the Bon religion, the indigenous belief of the land before Buddhism arrived in the seventh century. The Nakhi call him Dongba Shilo and hold him to be the father of the Dongba religion. They claim he underwent severe ascetic training here and received his spiritual powers here.

The cave itself is difficult to find. If you attempt the climb, expect to take three hours for the round-trip. Rely on local guides or woodcutters to direct you to the mouth of the cave. The interior is bare save for some recent Dongba writing on the walls. Some call this place the Cave of the Ancient Sorcerer.

The mountain dominating this part of Zhongdian is named Haba, a magnificent, perennially snowcapped peak that rises to 5396 metres (17,700 feet).

BITA HAI AND NAPA HAI

These lakes and their surrounding nature preserves have become popular one or two-day trips for local and foreign tourists. Bita Hai lies 25 kilometres east of Zhongdian; it is the smaller and more visited of the two. At approximately the 23 kilometre mark from Zhongdian on the road to Baishuitai, a road goes to the left. Take this road for 500 metres to a point where the trail to Bita Hai begins.

Napa is a huge lake. The main road north towards Benzilan passes it a few kilometres beyond Zhongdian; the water spreads away far below while yaks graze at the shore.

BENZILAN

Benzilan, two hours by car from Zhongdian, is a pleasant town standing at 1968 metres on a narrow strip of land on the right bank of the Upper Yangzi, tucked between water and sharply rising hills. It is a waystation on the main road north, halfway between Zhongdian and Deqen; the road passes above the farms, wooden houses and small temples of the town. The busy strip of Sichuan style restaurants is constantly visited by cars, trucks and buses. Sichuan Province and the village of Wake (Dongfent) lie just across the water but can only be reached by a ferry.

Near the south of town, below the road, is Göchen Gompa, a small Tibetan temple with pretty murals. Walking north through the fields and lanes brings one to a stupa, always visited by old men and pious women, and another *gompa*.

DONGZHULIN MONASTERY

Twenty-two kilometres north of Benzilan on the main road is Dongzhulin Monastery, the second large Yellow Hat centre in northwestern Yunnan. It was rebuilt at this conspicuous spot for reasons of convenience; building materials could be brought to the site directly by truck. The old monastery, destroyed in 1959, stood 10 kilometres from here on a remote mountain. Dongzhulin today has 300 monks and a *tulku* (incarnate lama) named Shumba Tenzing Chenling Choyöng.

Deqen

Deqen is Yunnan's northernmost county, most of which borders Sichuan, but a part in the west abuts Tibet. This border with Tibet is created by a massive mountain wall, running from north to south, known as the Kawa Karpo Range. Its tallest peak, called Meili Xue Shan in Chinese, is the province's highest point at 6,740 metres. The dramatic gorge of the Mekong River defines the range's eastern base. Numerous mountaineering expeditions have assaulted the main peak, but all have failed. In the beginning of 1991, seventeen Japanese and Chinese climbers died in a single avalanche. Experienced and worldly mountaineers consider this region to

CHINA'S LONG-NECKED CRANES
By *Wong How-Man*

Throughout Chinese history, the crane has been considered very auspicious. The stately position that it holds is perhaps only rivalled by the mythical dragon. Indeed the crane is often called 'Xian He', or heavenly crane, by the Chinese. From motifs of the Imperial Palace in Beijing to the simple New Year posters on the wall of a peasant's home in the far-off countryside, the symbol of the crane graces every corner of Chinese life.

Its elegant form has long been praised by poets and its every graceful movement depicted by the fine brushstrokes of artists. Indeed, many Chinese idioms and legends revolve around the crane. As a very important part of Chinese culture, the crane has come to represent longevity and prosperity. Their courtship and pairing activities have come to symbolize a long and stable relationship.

Scientifically there are 15 species of crane in the world, of which China has nine. One species that stands out among the rest is the Black-necked Crane (*Grus nigricollis*). It is the only crane that spends its entire life cycle on the high plateau. Mating and breeding during the summer in Tibet and Qinghai, the Black-necked Crane descend to the slightly lower elevation of Yunnan and Guizhou provinces during the winter.

It is during the harsh winter months that the cranes face their greatest challenges from man. As the birds flock together in larger numbers, they are more susceptible to interference by man's activities, be it poaching, habitat loss or degradation. There are also inherent conflicts as the cranes forage in the fields of the farmers.

It is with such resolve that Shell China is supporting an endeavour by the Hong Kong-based China Exploration & Research Society to alleviate such conflicts. At present, an integrated program is in place at Xundian County, the southernmost wintering site of the Black-necked Cranes.

The program includes publicity to local villagers regarding the state-protected status of the cranes, revival of the traditional belief of the crane among the Chinese, inclusion of field trips and teaching curriculum about cranes into area schools, introduction of birdwatching tours to boost local economy, reward for reported poaching activities, set up of county-level reserve, and control of wetland habitat.

Early results after the first year of conservation activities showed that the wintering crane population has stabilized. As pairing cranes are recognised for their long and stable relationship with each other, we hope that such a relationship will be an inspiration for man to live in harmony with the nature around him.

be one of Nature's grandest displays, an enormous land cut by tremendous rivers that form some of the Earth's deepest gorges.

Deqen is also the name of the county seat, formerly known as Atuntze. Like most Tibetan towns, it has an old, traditional section and a new, faceless concrete section that mimicks Chinese settlements. The old town, to the north, is a pleasure, with solid wooden houses and yaks in the alleyways. Deqen has 45 Moslem families; these are Tibetan Moslems, not Hui Chinese. They were mostly linked to the caravan trade that once transported tea, wool, gold, medicines and cloth to and from Lhasa and India. A 'fast' route from Deqen to Sadiya in Assam took only 18 days.

A visit to Deqen should be made for the grand landscapes, mighty mountains and spectacular descents to the river valleys. Buddhist monasteries still exist both close to town and in remote fastnesses.

NAKA TRASHI TEMPLE

Between Deqen and the Kawa Karpo lookout point is the important Tibetan temple of Naka Trashi. Chinese translate the name of this place as Fei Lai Si, 'the temple that flew from afar'. It is considered an eastern anchor of Tibetan religious civilization, and as such it is visited by thousands of pilgrims. Kawa Karpo, White Guardian of the holy mountain, is enshrined here as a statue, riding a white horse with the white mountain rising up under his steed.

DECHENLING MONASTERY

Dechenling is a newly reconstructed *gompa* (monastery) on the outskirts of Deqen, next to the road that descends to the Mekong and Yanmen. The incarnate lama from here is in exile in India. It is a Yellow Hat institution that suffered destruction in the late 1950s. A few fine murals remain, painted on boards that survived nearly four decades of neglect.

Western Yunnan

From Dali to Ruili

The long journey from Dali to Ruili on the Burmese border traverses the ancient Yongchang Route, southwestern end of the Southwest Silk Road. Yongchang is the ancient name of Baoshan, midway point along the route.

After Xiaguan, the first large town is Yongping, 105 kilometres to the west, once a staging post for caravans before they crossed the Bonan Mountains. This stretch was made by conscript labour from the time of the Han Emperor Wudi (105 BC). In 69 BC, the route was further expanded under Emperor Mingdi. Workers from that time created a song, which has come to be known as 'Leading to Bonan'.

> To climb over the hills of Bonan,
>
> We knock and knock rocks, ding and dang,
>
> Day and night.
>
> Defying death to cross the Lanjin Ferry,
>
> We fly over the Lancang River.
>
> What do we get for all this suffering?
>
> We suffer so that others can sing for joy.

Bonan Shan (2800 metres), lies between Yongping to the east and the Mekong River (Lancang Jiang) to the west. The song's reference to Lanjin Ferry is the site of Rainbow Bridge (see page 110), which collapsed in 1986 because of floods. Now bamboo rafts have returned to ferry people and goods across the Mekong. The road continues to Baoshan, an old and important crossroad.

BAOSHAN

After Xiaguan, Baoshan is the largest city in western Yunnan, an industrial and transport centre. From the third century onwards, it has been important for trade, formerly exchanging gold, precious stones, peacocks, rhinoceroses, elephants and silk with India and the countries of Southeast Asia. Indian merchants settled here during the Tang Dynasty. Baoshan has been a cloth making centre for centuries and today continues to produce materials made from sisal and kapok.

Two Buddhist sites worth mentioning are in the area. Fifteen kilometres north of town are the Yunyan Mountains where one can find rock sculptures of a 'reclining' Buddha (depiction of the Buddha's death and entrance into Nirvana) and Five Hundred Arhats. The Buddha is reputed to be from the early Eighth century.

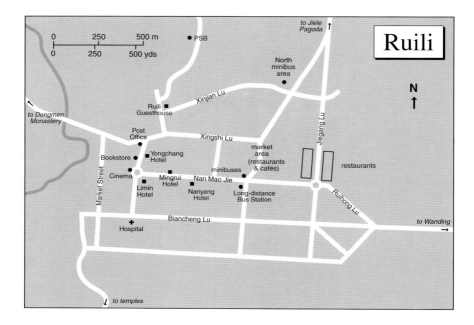

Guangzun Si, a monastary erected in the Tang Dynasty, contains four courtyards of halls and pavilions. Although repaired many times, it is the oldest preserved site in Baoshan. In the west part of the city, near the Teacher's College, is a Qing-Dynasty pagoda. The 16th-century Yuhuang (Jade Emperor) Pavilion, now the Cultural Relics Bureau, has gaudy murals of the Jade Emperor but fine architecture and a worthy ceiling.

West of Baoshan lie the Gaoligong Shan, a huge range running all the way north to the borders of Tibet. At a place called Zhuge Liang City, an old garrison town, the historic Southwest Silk Road split. The main branch went to Tengchong and Myitkyina in Burma, the other to Mangshi and Lashio.

The main route from Baoshan angles southwest towards Mangshi (Luxi), crossing the grand Salween River (Nu Jiang) after 90 kilometres. The valley of the Salween is nothing short of magnificent, with its deep cut lying between high, verdant mountains. Crops are everywhere: corn, buckwheat, potatoes, sugar cane, papaya, coffee.

Mangshi, also known as Luxi, is the capital of the Dehong Dai Jingpo Autonomous Prefecture, 200 km from Baoshan. The Dai people of Dehong are often called Land Dai, as opposed to the Water Dai of Xishuangbanna.

An airport here has flights to and from Kunming. Numerous small temples dot the town and a Tree-Embracing Pagoda actually has a tree as part of its structure.

The true Burma road continues from Mangshi to Wanding and then leaves China by crossing over the Mangshi River into Burma. Wanding was once an important trade centre; now the action has moved west to Ruili, 30 kilometres away.

TENGCHONG

In the first decades of this century, the main route from Dali to Burma crossed the Mekong River, went through Baoshan, continued west-

The White Pagoda, Damenglong

ward over the great Salween River and reached Tengchong (formerly Tengyueh). The building of the Burma Road in the late 1930s shifted the route farther south, from Baoshan to Luxi (Mangshi) and on to Wanding, bypassing Tengchong; this today remains the primary highway in western Yunnan.

Tengchong, though a small city, has been home to many Burmese and 'Overseas Chinese' from Burma and is a historic trading town. It opened to foreign trade in the Qing Dynasty and was deemed important enough by the British to establish a Consulate there; the first consul arrived in 1899 and the office remained open until well into the 1940s. The city has much of the feel of Yunnan 15 or 20 years ago, with winding, cobblestone streets in the old quarter, wooden buildings and high, walled compounds.

Old British Consulate: The former British Consulate building stands in the north-west part of Tengchong, beyond the large gate of the Municipal Foodstuffs compound (Liangshi Bu). It is unmistakeable, with its huge, barn-like roof and slightly upturned eaves. Look in and you will see that it has become a warehouse for grain, oil and liquor. Remnants of an old map are on the top floor. This impressive building was constructed in 1916.

Henshun Village: Five kilometres west of Tengchong is a perfectly preserved village with outstanding examples of stone and wooden architecture. The centrepiece is the Heshun Library, built and supported by Overseas Chinese. It was established in 1924 and contains over 70,000 books. The library was made from the best materials and workmanship of the time. It opens at 8am each morning.

Mountains and Volcanoes: Western Yunnan is a zone of volcanic and subterranean thermal activity. North of Tengchong is a minor wonderland of some 100 volcanic cones that dot a broad plain. Forty-three kilometres north of the city is the Gaoligong Shan Nature Reserve with its beautiful peaks and forests. Nearby is Yunfeng Shan, a Daoist mountain that retains remnants of late Ming and early Qing temples and pavilions.

RUILI

The proper name for Ruili is the Burmese 'Shweli'; the title Foggy City comes from the Dai language. In the past six years Ruili has become a fast-growing, rough-and-tumble boom town with arrivals every day from all over China, people with a dream of finding work or finding riches. It is common in a restaurant or gathering to find Chinese from Liaoning, Shandong, Fujian, Guangdong or Sichuan. Burmese with short-term travel permits stream into Ruili, most to conduct petty trade or find a buyer for a few gems and pieces of jade. Arms dealers and drug men are here, too. Bangladeshis, Nepalis and Pakistanis occasionally turn up.

The street markets themselves are wonderful and strange, filled with Burmese hustlers, Mandalay rum, elephant's trunk in slices (dried), python skins, tortoise shells, bear's gall, false pearls, swords, prostitutes and betel-nut sellers. Culture seems to be at a low ebb in this kind of town, though there is energy, plenty of fun and good feeling for those who are open to the rag-tag mix of people who have come here to seek their fortunes. (A map of Ruili can be found on page 156.)

The Dehong Dai, distant kin to the Dai of Xishuangbanna, have a number of temples and monasteries in the Ruili area. The Buddhism practiced here is Theravada (Way of the Elders), also known as southern Buddhism. Influence from Burma is strong on the Buddhism of the Dais: Golden Duck Temple, southwest of Ruili; Hansha Temple, farther west of Ruili; Denghanlong Temple, past Jiexing; Leizhuang Ta, a pagoda; Jiele Jin Ta, 'golden pagoda', east of Ruili; Xiao Guanyin Si, 'Small Goddess of Mercy Temple', the only Mahayana Buddhist site in Ruili. All architecture and decorations are in local style.

BORDER CROSSINGS

The border regions of Yunnan, especially the tracts near Vietnam and Burma, have a growing reputation for lawlessness and crime. It is prudent to stay alert when in these areas, watch you possessions and develop a sixth sense about possible danger. In the Ruili area there are three major border crossings into Burma: from Nongdao to Namkham, from Ruili to Muse and from Wanding across the Shuili River. In the Xishuangbanna area, the main crossings are from Mengla to Namtha in Laos and, farther west, from Daluo to Burma. Much farther to the east, Yunnan's narrow gauge railway leads all the way from Kunming to the border at Hekou. The Vietnamese town opposite Hekou is Laocai.

Xishuangbanna

Yunnan's southernmost region, bordering Burma and Laos, is officially known as the Xishuangbanna Dai Autonomous Prefecture. The Dai are one of Yunnan's major minority groups, numbering nearly 850,000 throughout the province; nearly a third of these reside in Xishuangbanna. This long and evocative name is actually a sinicized form of the Dai *Sipsong bana* which simply means 'twelve administrative units', a nomenclature from the late 16th century.

Xishuangbanna lies just below the Tropic of Cancer. It is a marvellously rich and fecund area, holding fully one quarter of China's faunal species and one-sixth of its plant species. There are only two seasons here, hot and dry, and hot and wet. Monsoon rains usually arrive in June, are heaviest in August and September, and finally let up in October.

In the past, rain, humidity, heat and isolation, combined with actual diseases, earned Xishuangbanna the grim sobriquet 'land of lethal vapours'. Any man planning a trip there was strongly advised to say a final goodbye to his wife and get a coffin ready. Malaria and cholera were perennial killers, and in 1929 bubonic plague wiped out a large section of the population. Since the 1950s, steady progress has been made in public health and, with the rare exception of some malaria, it is now perfectly safe to travel in Xishuangbanna.

The early history of the Dai is lost to an ancient, pre-literate age, but there are clearly linguistic and cultural links between these graceful, slim-waisted people and those in Thailand. The questions of common ancestry and migration have not been conclusively answered, however, and many theories, some self-serving and nationalistic, continue to contradict one another.

A lyrical origination story stands firmly in the hearts of the people. In the beginning Xishuangbanna was a vast ocean which in time subsided to reveal a lush and bountiful paradise. The Dai flourished and wanted for nothing until jealous demons waged bloody war and seized the land. Awful slaughter and misery descended, birds and insects ceased their music-making and even the light of day disappeared. The land was plunged into total darkness.

This impossible situation was challenged by a brave and resolute young man who led his people in a life-and-death struggle against the demons. The enemy was forced to retreat and the demon-king leapt into the Mekong River to escape. The tireless youth pursued and they fought a seven-day battle beneath the rushing water. Victory came at last and the Dai hero emerged with a magical pearl taken from the demon's throat. He hung this high in a tree where its radiance lit up the land, and to this very day the capital of Xishuangbanna is called Jinghong, the City of Dawn, in remembrance of that mythical day.

The first actual records appear in the second century BC, when the Han Dynasty acknowledged tributary missions from Dai chieftains. From the eighth to 13th centuries, Xishuangbanna was incorporated into the Nanzhao and Dali Kingdoms, and only after that time did it become a vassal of China, one of the empire's most godforsaken outposts. In 1570 a Ming Bureau of Pacification was established to intensify control over border areas; this style of administration continued well into the Qing Dynasty, but as the Manchu world became increasingly moribund in the late 19th century, colonial powers stepped in. First France, with its neighbouring Indo-Chinese territories, toyed with encroachment and then Britain actually occupied Jinghong with a force of 500 troops. In the end, however, both powers decided to keep Xishuangbanna as a buffer zone.

During the first half of the 20th century, Xishuangbanna was controlled by a Chinese warlord and by an ancient, stifling system imposed by indigenous overlords. For the common people, 'the water they drank, the road they walked on, the quarters they dwelled in, the very earth which covered their faces at death' were all subject to taxation.

The People's Liberation Army entered Xishuangbanna in 1950 but was not greeted as heir to the Legend of the Pearl. Rather, the Dai mistrusted the Chinese soldiers and saw them as a new wave of oppressors. In time confidence grew between both groups and, despite cruelties during the Cultural Revolution, Han-Dai relations are good and Xishuangbanna is one of the most successfully integrated minority areas in China.

Getting to Xishuangbanna

The commonest way to reach Xishuangbanna is by taking the daily flight from Kunming to the airport at Jinghong and then boarding an airport bus for the short 15-minute ride into Xishuangbanna's capital.

Formerly, flights south from Kunming went only to Simao, capital of the Simao District. This way can still be undertaken by the adventuresome traveller. The 165-kilometre (103-mile) overland trip from Simao to Jinghong takes four to five hours along a paved, mountain road. At the 33-kilometre (20-mile) marker there is a checkpoint for all vehicles passing from Simao District into Xishuangbanna's Jinghong County. After this the road rambles on, occasionally traversing narrow plains of rice and sugar cane, with tea and rubber growing on hillsides near the villages. But parts of the trip cut through Rousseau-like jungles, lush and overflowing, filled with impenetrable greenery. The road finally comes out high above a river valley and then rapidly descends towards the huge yellow bends of the silt-filled Mekong River. Jinghong lies on its west bank.

The Simao District Guesthouse (Simao Diqu Zhaodaisuo) is where foreigners usually stay if they choose to come this way. It has a good dining room; local specialities include fried wasp larva, steamed frog, monkey liver and a strong, sweet, piquant corn brew.

There are two main ways to pass a few hours in Simao. One is to visit the Plum River Reservoir Park (Meizihe Shuiku Gongyuan), 7 kilometres (4.5 miles) south-

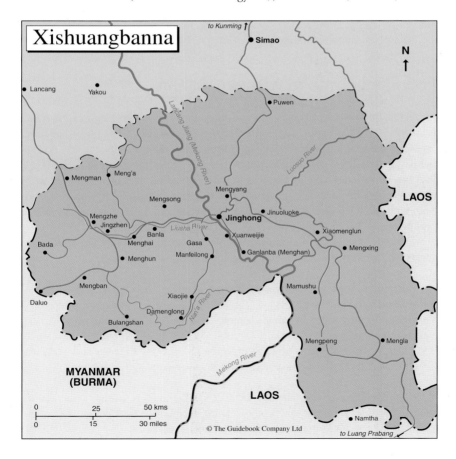

east of the town. Here there are paddle boats, clean water and quiet surroundings—a good place to swim or relax. The second way is to explore Simao on foot and discover the old wooden town, secreted away behind the broad, dusty main thoroughfares. The old houses and cobbled alleys crowd together on a hill east of the main north-south road. There you can see little teashops, beautifully carved lintels and window frames, stacks of firewood, pack animals—in short, a way of life that is rapidly being usurped by modernization and new construction.

An alternative way to reach Jinghong from Kunming is to make the entire trip by bus, a 740-kilometre (462-mile) journey. The quickest route takes two days, passing through Yuxi, Eshan, Mojiang, Simao and Mengyang and requires spending a night along the way in a small hostel or guesthouse. Tickets for this long-distance bus can be bought at the main Passenger Transport Bus Station on Beijing Lu, near the railway station in Kunming.

Food and Drink in Xishuangbanna

Xishuangbanna's tropical climate allows for a rich variety of delicious, exotic food. Fruit lovers will be happy here with a changing seasonal collection of bananas, papayas, mangoes, pineapples, lychees, jackfruits, breadfruits and many others. The Dai pay special attention to their rice, its texture, size, colour, taste and 'perfume'. Two special varieties are glutinous rice (*nuomi*), generally cooked in a mould with meat, fish, egg or sweet filling, similar to Chinese rice dumplings (*zhongzi*), and *zimi,* a purple-hued rice much prized for its colour and flavour, steamed inside a cylindrical section of bamboo.

If you are invited to a Dai house for a meal, or want to arrange a visit through a travel agency, a typical menu might include the following dishes:

- Zucchini (courgettes) with special fragrant herbs
- Mild pickled bamboo shoots
- Minced meat steamed in banana leaves
- Fish in a thick sauce with garlic sprouts
- *Qingta,* crisp fried sheets of water vegetable
- *Biandou,* a large, flat bean served with tomato puree

- Spicy chicken
- Pea-shoot soup
- Sesame beef
- Fried banana
- Sweets and green tea

All of the above are accompanied by overflowing bowls of strong, white liquor. Such an evening, sitting in low bamboo chairs, surrounded by friendly people, listening to the soft night noises, is an unforgettable experience.

Sights in Xishuangbanna

JINGHONG

The small capital of Xishuangbanna, despite its broad avenues and Chinese-style cement buildings, has all the feelings of an upland Southeast Asian town. There is an unhurried ease here that has charm if your expectations are in tempo with the place. As the head of the local Foreign Affairs Bureau says, 'There is really not much going on here'.

He is not entirely correct. Foreign visitors invariably leave Xishuangbanna with a quizzical sense of having been to a special place, far from the crush of China proper, a land filled with kind, gentle people.

Jinghong comes alive on market and festival days, but for the most part its commercial life is limited to the shops along the main street, with their weird assortment of goods, and to the rows of outdoor vendors in the northern part of town— watch and bicycle repairmen, clothing stalls, hat sellers and fruiterers. Minority clothing and crafts are available in the markets.

Jinghong is a good place for strolling, whether it be down to the banks of the Mekong River or southward to the traditional Dai stilt-housed villages that make up the suburbs. Jinghong is the base and starting point for all excursions into the hinterlands of Xishuangbanna.

TROPICAL CROPS RESEARCH INSTITUTE

In the western suburbs of Jinghong lies the Tropical Crops Research Institute, a large, well laid out estate with a beautiful palm-lined entranceway. Its staff of 1,300 look after the grounds and conduct research in a number of fields related to economic plants. The institute manages a vast rubber plantation that contributes significantly to its annual revenues. Tapping of the rubber trees begins at the end of March and continues uninterrupted for nine months, at which time the trees need to rest.

In the midst of the rubber forest is a large concrete memorial. Every visitor to the institute will be told the story of how, on 14 April 1961, Premier Zhou Enlai met with Premier U Nu at this spot to discuss the Sino-Burmese border situation.

Within sight of the main building are long gardens containing dozens of plant species with economic and medicinal importance to man. Pepper, oil palm, cinnamon, cocoa pods, nutmeg and sesame are here in abundance.

WATER SPLASHING FESTIVAL (POSHUI JIE)

The Dai Lunar New Year, commonly called the Water Splashing Festival, is marked each April by three days of unbridled celebration, drunkenness and hilarity. It is a

The Land of the Blue Poppy

The Mekong Valley

*T*he weather had now set in fine, and nothing could have been more delightful than these marches up the Mekong valley, for we took matters fairly easily, making four stages from Hsiao-wei-hsi to Tsu-kou. Sometimes the narrow path was enveloped in the shade of flowering shrubs and walnut trees, the branches breasting us as we rode, the air sweetened by the scent of roses which swept in cascades of yellow flowers over the summits of trees thirty feet high; sometimes we plunged into a deep limestone gorge, its cliffs festooned with ferns and orchids, our caravan climbing up by rough stone steps which zigzagged backwards and forwards till we were out of ear-shot of the rapids in the river below; sometimes the path was broken altogether by a scree-shoot, which, dangerous as it looked, the mules walked across very calmly, though sending rocks grinding and sliding down through the trees into the river.

In one gorge through which we passed, large pot-holes were visible across the river between winter and summer water marks and yet others still higher up, forming a conspicuous feature of the otherwise smooth bare cliffs which dipped sheer into the river; but on the left or shaded bank dense vegetation prevailed wherever tree, shrub, or rock-plant could secure a foothold. The further north we went the more rich and varied became the vegetation of the rainy belt, though the paucity of forest trees, except deep down in the gullies, was always conspicuous.

Shales and slates, dipping at very high angles, and often vertical, alternated with limestone, through which the river had cut its way straight downwards; but at one spot, where an enormous rapid had been formed, huge boulders of a dark-green volcanic rock, like lava, with large included fragments, lined the shore and were piled in confusion below cliffs of slate.

It is at sunset that the charm of this wonderful valley is displayed at its best, for the sun having dropped out of sight behind the western range still sends shafts of coloured light pulsing down the valley, rose, turquoise, and pale-green slowly chasing each other across the sky till darkness sets in and the stars sparkle gloriously. It is long after dawn when the sleeping valley wakens to floods of sunlight again, and the peaks which stand setinel over it, blotting out the views to north and south, lose the ghastly grey pallor of dimly-lit snow.

A Tibetan Festival

The Tibetan festival itself seemed more in accord with the usages of nat propitiation than with lamaism, except that it was eminently cheerful, and the people, led by their priests, went to the summits of the three nearest hills to east, north, and west in turn, in order to burn incense and pray; after which they ate cakes. The first day however was devoted entirely to the amusement of the children, for Tibetan mothers, as I frequently observed, are warm-hearted creatures with a great affection for their offspring.

Dressed in their best frocks, and wearing all the family jewels brought out for the occasion, they went up into the woods in the afternoon, picked bunches of flowers just as English children love to do, romped, made swings and swung each other, and finally sat down to eat cakes, which they had been busily making for a week past.

Just as the young of different animals more nearly resemble each other than do the adults, so too are children very much alike in their games the world over; picnicking is not confined to Hampstead Heath, nor picking flowers to botanists.

In the evening they all trooped back to the village to dance in the mule square, and skip. Three of four little girls would link arms and facing another similar line of girls advance and retreat by turns, two steps and a kick, singing, in spite of their harsh voices, a not unmusi cal chorus; the other side would then reply, and so it went on, turn and turn about.

The Last of the Mekong

This was the last we were destined to see of the great Mekong river. I was scarcely sorry to say goodbye, for the Mekong gorge—one long ugly rent between mountains which grow more and more arid, more and more savage as we travel northwards (yet hardly improve as we travel southwards)—is an abnormality, a grim freak of nature, a thing altogether out of place. Perhaps I had not been sufficiently ill-used by this extraordinary river to have a deep affection for it. The traveller, buffeted and bruised by storm and mountain, cherishes most the foe worthy of his steel. Nevertheless there was a strange fascination about its olive-green water in winter, its boiling red floods in summer, and the everlasting thunder of its rapids. And its peaceful little villages, some of them hidden away in the dips between the hills, others straggling over sloping alluvial fans or perched up on some ancient river-terrace where scattered blocks of stone suggest the decay of a ruined civiliza-tion—all these oases break the depressing monotony of naked rock and ill-nourished vegetation, delighting the eye with the beauty of their ver-dure and the richness of their crops.

Happy people! What do they know of the strife and turmoil of the western world? We wear ourselves out saving time in one direction that we may waste it in another, hurrying and ever hurrying through time as if we were disgusted with life, but these people think of time not in miles an hour but according to the rate at which their crops grow in the spring, and their fruits ripen in the autumn. They work that they and their families may have enough to eat and enough to wear, living and dying where they were born, where their offspring will live and die after them, as did their ancestors before them, shut in by the mountains which bar access from the outer world.

Frank Kingdon-Ward, Himalayan Enchantment, 1990

wonderful time to be in Xishuangbanna, if you do not mind a vast crush of people and a shortage of all services.

The festival is similar to Thailand's Songkran celebration and has its origin rooted in the theme of titanic struggle between the forces of good and evil. As the story goes, the Dai people were subjugated by demons who possessed magical forces. The demon-king had seven beautiful consorts, the last of whom was a kind-hearted lady who wanted to help her people. One evening, by plying the wicked king with drink and feigning loving concern, she extracted the secret of his vul-

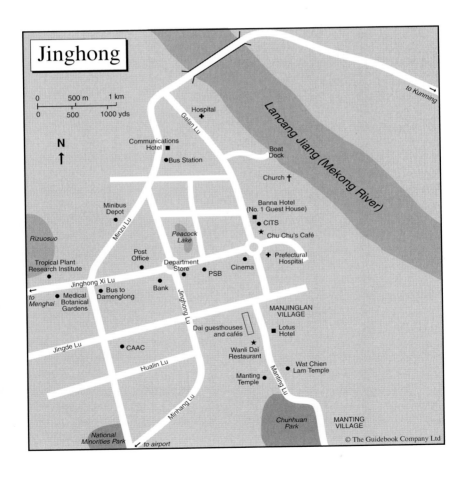

nerability. His neck was tender and weak—he could be strangled easily. When the demon-king dozed off, the brave maiden plucked a single white hair from his head, wrapped it around his neck and pulled with all her might. Not only did the king die, but his head came off entirely and to everyone's dismay erupted into a violent fountain of froth, blood and fire. Flames threatened to engulf the entire land so in desperation each of the seven women took turns holding the head while the others poured water on it to wash away the blood and quell the flames. The spell was finally broken, peace and tranquillity returned to the land and ever since the people have celebrated the Water Splashing Festival, to honour their release and to wash away the sins, ignorance and obstacles of the previous year.

Today, despite opposition from many local Dai, the government has standardized the date of the festival rather then letting it range over weeks as it did in the past. It is fixed for 13–18 April, with three main days of activities. These include fiercely competitive dragon-boat races on the river, parades, giant skyrockets, songs in thc streets, buffalo slaughter, with much eating and drinking and splashing water everywhere. It is impossible to stay dry; be careful of your camera.

The outstanding feature of the Water Splashing Festival is the gathering of so many different minority groups in one place, all dressed in their finest clothing, for several joyous days of singing, dancing and revelry.

MENGHAI

Travelling from Jinghong through the valley of the Flowing Sands River (Liusha He) brings one to Menghai, one of the rare broad plains of Xishuangbanna, a region of 'bounty and delight' for the Dai people. Menghai's relatively high altitude of 1,400 metres (4,600 feet) limits it to one rice crop per year but the weather is perfect for tea. This is one of the great tea regions of China, providing Hong Kong with most of its beloved *pu'er (bolei)* tea, Tibet with essential tea bricks, and France with a popular and profitable tea for slimming, *tuocha*. The Menghai Tea Factory (Menghai Chachang) is the largest industrial employer in Xishuangbanna. Arrangements to visit the tea factory can be made through travel agencies.

Menghai, a dusty market town, lies 53 kilometres (33 miles) west of Jinghong and has simple accommodations for visitors.

OCTAGONAL PAGODA (BAJIAOTING)

Under the guise of different names, thc Octagonal Pagoda is the most famous architectural site in Xishuangbanna. It stands on a man-made hill 14 kilometres (8 miles) west of Menghai, just off the main road, near Jingzhen Village; it is also known as Jingzhen Pagoda (Jingzhenta).

The story of the temple's construction revolves around two pious locals who

Traditional house, Xishuangbanna

wanted simultaneously to honour the Buddha and put an end to a tyranny of marauding wasps. Between the years 1698-1701 they supervised the construction of a wasp-displacing hill, built the temple and encouraged religious gatherings. Their masterpiece, renovated four times, is now a protected cultural monument. The temple has an overall feeling of compactness, intricacy and richness. Its heavy coloured base of alternating hues—blue, yellow, green, red and glass-covered stripes—anchors the brick bottom to the earth. Higher up on a deep, reddish-brown background, gold designs of flowers, stupas, trees, *dharma* wheels, *chakras* and geometric forms create an interim level. Finally, the fantastic eight-sectioned, ten-tiered roof rises steeply to a round, scaloped cupola, topped by a Buddha-spire of hoops and dangling metal objects. Careful scrutiny will reveal many details and mythical beasts on the 16-metre (53-foot) -high pagoda.

Three surrounding buildings on the hilltop, built in 1985, now house a library and living quarters for the local monks. Notice the amusing and touching paintings on the wall of the library, done in a simple, folk style to show sacred animals, pious tales and stories from the Buddha's former lives.

MENGZHE

Nearly 20 kilometres (14 miles) beyond Menghai lies the town of Mengzhe, in the heart of tea growing country. There are several pagodas in the area; the best known is Manlei Great Buddha Pagoda, with two large painted stupas. The central one rises 20 metres (66 feet) from a square base. The main body of the stupa is a heavy, tapering cylinder, topped with a spire and intricate filigree. The 700-Buddha Temple is here in Mengzhe as well.

DALUO

Daluo lies in the southwesternmost corner of Menghai County, a mere two kilometres from the border with Burma. Chinese tourists come here for the thrill of a border crossing; the place itself is a dusty frontier town of two main streets, lots of construction, temporary shanties and the hope and squalor of all such places. A daily market is the place to see many minorities, some coming from or going to Burma for buying and selling.

The road from Menghai is good and passes through lowland and mountain homes of the Hani and Bulang.

BANLA HANI VILLAGE

After the Dai, the Hani (Aini) People are the most common minority group in Xishuangbanna. A stop at Banla is the easiest way to see a mountain village in its naturalness and material simplicity. Although overburdened by foreigners because of its closeness to the main Jinghong-Menghai road, the Hani (Aini) here will not flaunt their 'ethnicity'. Visitors are advised to be circumspect and polite after crossing the Flowing Sands River into Hani territory. A path leads upward past the houses into mountains beyond, affording a beautiful view in several directions if you climb high enough.

Banla lies 37 kilometres (23 miles) west of Jinghong.

KING OF TEA TREES AT NANNUOSHAN

A road leads south from the main road, 35 kilometres (21 miles) west of Jinghong. It climbs steadily up Nannuoshan for 8 kilometres (5 miles) to a small, flat clearing, the point of departure for a long, 817-step descent by foot to the King of Tea Trees. This 800-year-old botanical wonder is reputed to have been planted by ancestors of the local Aini minority. It stands 5.5 metres (18 feet) and helps support the theory that all tea in the world originated in southern Yunnan Province.

In most areas of China, rice grows submerged in water but some varieties, known as upland rice, grow in the earth with little or no irrigation. Nannuoshan gets its name, Southern Glutinous Rice Mountain, from the type of rice that is cultivated on its slopes by the Aini people. Farther up the mountain live the Lahu in clustered villages.

THE MEKONG RIVER (LANCANGJIANG) AND OLIVE PLAIN (GANLANBA)

The mighty Mekong, third longest river in China and 13th longest in the world, surges through the middle of Xishuangbanna, past Jinghong and onward to Laos. It is spanned at only a few points; one of these is the vital Jinghong Bridge, built in 1960 to link the entire region by road with Kunming.

The Mekong is navigable for nearly 320 kilometres (200 miles) inside Yunnan, but for visitors there is one main river trip southward to the huge agricultural farm of the Olive Plain (Ganlanba). A boat leaves every morning from under the big bridge for the one-hour trip downstream. Early morning mists frequently obscure the scenery but, in the afternoon, the longer return voyage upstream is almost always clear. Public buses leave each morning from Jinghong's main bus station and travel down the east bank of the Mekong to the Olive Plain.

Large plantations of rubber and fruit trees cover the expansive plain; they are interspersed with brilliant emerald rice fields, random groves of coconut palms and occasional tea fields. The local Dai people call the area Menghan, which is also the name of the main town. Here daily markets attract a variety of minority groups from

The many faces of the people of Yunnan

the surrounding countryside. Han Chinese, though certainly evident, only began settling in southern Xishuangbanna in the late 1950s.

The serenity of the Olive Plain is best experienced by walking from village to village, under large trees and along shaded paths which lead past ample wooden houses on stilts. There is always a scene of peaceful activity by the river; women washing, children playing or fetching water, fishing boats returning home with their catch.

In the village of Manting the Weijiang Baita pagoda is a historically important religious structure that dates back to the 12th century. It was considered one of the finest Burmese-style pagodas in China. Tragedy struck during the 1960s when Red Guards used dynamite to blow it up. The present huge structure was completed in March 1985 but the craftsmanship in no way approaches its predecessor. Other pagodas are scattered about the Olive Plain.

There are simple but adequate hotels in Menghan for tourists who want to stay for several days, and numerous small restaurants along the main market street.

DAMENGLONG AND THE WHITE AND BLACK PAGODAS (BAITA, HEITA)

Southwest of Jinghong, only 8 kilometres (5 miles) from Burma, lies the village of Damenglong and its well-known pagodas. The 70-kilometre (44-mile) trip takes two hours on rough roads though stops along the way can turn this outing into a full-day trip.

The first sight, just beyond the turn-off from the main highway, is Manguanglong Monastery, where it is possible to see the life of a religious community, with 30 or so young Buddhist monks and their two caring, yet stern, teachers who look after the education and development of the boys. The entranceway is flanked by two long undulating dragons. The dominant building is a temple hall for prayer and recitation from lontar-palm sutras. It houses a large, crude Buddha statue and many strips of white and coloured cloth offerings.

If you visit the monastery, there are certain rules of courtesy to follow: do not touch the heads of monks; do not expose the soles of your shoes or feet in the direction of a person; take your shoes off when entering a temple; always respect the image of the Buddha and use care and discretion when taking photographs.

Down the road is Manfeilong Reservoir, a good place for boating or picnicking. From here, the route winds across the countryside, through valleys of rice, up and over hills covered with neat rows of rubber trees, past sections of jungle and eventu-

THE GEOLOGY OF SOUTHWEST CHINA

The geologic history of Southwest China is certainly one of the most fascinating, complex and scientifically important of any region in the world. By far the most significant event in shaping the major landforms of the area was the collision of the Indian subcontinent with Asia, some 40 to 50 million years ago. Driven by internal forces that are not yet fully understood, a dozen crustal fragments moved slowly across the surface of the Earth. The Indian plate traveled steadily northward at the rate of 15 to 20 centimeters per year, eventually closing the eastern arm of the ancient Sea of Tethys that once lay south of Tibet. It finally rammed into the Asian continent and caused 2,000 kilometers of crustal shortening and compression. India continues its relentless penetration into Asia, but at the slower rate of five centimeters per year.

This titanic collision created tight folds and overlapping crustal slices in the basement rocks of the Asian plate, thus forming the thickest crust (70–80 kilometers) and the highest mountains (the Himalaya) in the world. Mountain-building was not limited to the Himalaya, however, as the highlands of eastern Tibet, western Sichuan and northern Yunnan were all significantly affected. Today, signs of the rapid uplift in these areas can be seen in exceptionally deep gorges, with deposits of alluvial gravel perched several hundred meters above rivers that predated the collision. The rivers eroded downward as quickly as the mountains rose. A marvelous example of this is Tiger Leaping Gorge, where the Upper Yangzi River (Jinsha Jiang) has etched a spectacular gorge through 370 million-year-old Devonian marble, 4,000 meters beneath the ice and snow of Yulong Xue Shan, one of Yunnan's highest and most beautiful peaks.

The deformation of Asia as a result of the collision with India does not end here, however. To compensate for the continuing indentation, large blocks of China are slowly being driven outward on its unbounded sides into the basins of the South China Sea and the Pacific Ocean. The resulting horizontal movement has formed structural planes such as the Red River Fault in western Yunnan, along which the Red River now runs. This movement has caused the crust in Yunnan to pull apart and form grabens, extensive down-dropped areas. Some of these have filled with water to create large lakes, such as Dianchi near Kunming and Erhai near Dali.

Movement along the Red River and related faults has caused numerous high-magnitude earthquakes in Southwest China, some greater than 7.0 on the Richter scale. In addition, these faults allowed abnormally high heat flow to reach the surface of the Earth, creating the numerous hot springs in the region, and acted as conduits for the mineral-rich waters that helped deposit the well known gold reserves of Yunnan and western Sichuan. They appear, however, to have had little or no influence on the important deposits of iron, copper, lead, zinc, and tin in Yunnan, antimony in Guangxi and mercury in Guizhou.

The results of the collision with India have been superimposed on much older basement rocks that form the continental craton of Asia, the stable relatively immobile area of the Earth's crust. These deep basement rocks, as most others on the globe, do not comprise a homogeneous mass, but rather form a mixed collage of material that has increased in size over the past three billion years. Micro-continental fragments were welded together by global tectonic forces perhaps similar to those that are now driving the Indian plate. In fact, the cratonic basement of China consists of three large and several smaller blocks of Precambrian rock (older than 600 million years), fused together along suture zones. The large Precambrian block that underlies most of southern China is known as the Yangzi Craton. Surface exposures of these rocks are rare in southwest China and are usually limited to peripheral zones. In northern Guangxi, 2.86 billion-year-old granites can be observed along the southern cratonic border.

In contrast, the basement rocks that border the Yangzi Craton on the north and west, and which underlie Sichuan and western Yunnan, consist of folded rocks and micro-continental fragments that attached to the cratonic block, probably between 600 and 200 million years ago. An example of this, known as an accretionary fold belt, is the Sichuan Basin, formed by subsidence in an oceanic trench between 200 and 160 million years ago (Triassic-Jurassic). The basin first filled with a mixture of marine marl (clay and small organisms) and fine clastic sediments (fragments of pre-exisiting rocks) known as flysch. Later (140 to 100 million years ago), the basin was filled

with non-marine sandstone and conglomerate. These units now contain major deposits of coal and gas. The subsidence that generated these rocks in eastern Sichuan occurred long before the continental collision with India. The area was preserved as a structural basin throughout the subsequent periods of deformation because of its great distance from the point of initial collision.

A vast, shallow sea covered a major portion of the Yangzi Craton from early Cambrian through Triassic times (600 to 200 million years ago), depositing fossiliferous limestone throughout Guangxi, Guizhou and eastern Yunnan. Subsequent continental uplift and withdrawal of this sea left large areas of limestone exposed to the atmosphere. Where fractures in the limestone were numerous and rainfall abundant, acidic groundwater percolated downward and dissolved the limestone, forming caves, caverns and sinkholes. Formations such as these are common throughout southwest China. At certain localities where the limestone was particularly well fractured and soluble, the continuous dissolution by acidic groundwater caused underground holes to widen, ceilings of caverns to collapse, and numerous sinkholes to form in adjoining patterns. In time, the surface of the limestone terrain in such areas formed a network of numerous short gullies and ravines that terminated abruptly where they discharged their waters into subterranean channels. Erosion by wind and water continually reshaped the more resistant hills, leaving a spectacular collection of elongate and odd-shaped remnants of honey-combed chambers, passageways, caves and tunnels. Known as karst topography, this type of geomorphology gets its name from the Karst Mountains of Yugoslavia where it is particularly well developed.

Karst topography was formed in this manner at Yunnan's well-known Stone Forest, 126 kilometers southeast of Kunming. Here, elongate water channels, caves and passageways have been etched into 270 million-year-old Permian limestone. Even more spectacular, perhaps, are the exotically shaped karst formations naturally sculpted from 300 million-year-old Devonian limestone along the Lijiang River between Guilin and Yangshuo in Guangxi, truly a place where art and geology are one.

Taken from *Southwest China Off the Beaten Track*,
by K. Mark Stevens and George E. Wehrfritz, 1988

ally to Xiaogai, centre of the Dongfeng State Farm and host to a large Sunday market

Beyond Xiaogai, shortly before Damenglong, is Manfeilong on the right side of the road. Atop a hill behind this village stands White Pagoda, a 13th-century structure that has had innumerable restorations. It is now made largely of concrete, supported on two great concentric circular bases. Eight small stupas surround a taller, central spire. Local people describe the configuration, especially after a rainfall, as a cluster of spring bamboo shoots breaking through the earth as a vegetarian offering to the Buddha.

At the eastern base of the pagoda is a little red door. It stays locked most of the time but an old caretaker, if asked politely, will open the door to reveal a shrine overflowing with offerings of money, flowers, fruit and embroidered cloth. The object of devotion is a pair of oversized 'footprints of the Buddha', a religious constant throughout the Buddhist world, like splinters of the Original Cross to Christians.

The outside of the pagoda is painted in horizontal stripes of bright, primary colours with white designs, and is inlaid with chips of mirror. This gaudiness is offset by the overall grace and balance of the pagoda. For outrageous humor and crudeness, the side prayer hall has a bestiary of dragons, unicorns, lion-dogs and a comical elephant. The White Pagoda is perhaps the finest example of a Burmese-style pagoda in Xishuangbanna, along with one in Mengla.

In the distance, across a small valley just south of Damenglong, can be seen another pagoda. This is the undistinguished Black Pagoda, in fact a dirty-white structure with one main stupa and four smaller ones on the corners of a square concrete base. Clumsy workmanship is everywhere, but the tinkling bells and isolation, fine view and cool breezes afford some redemption for the effort of climbing to this spot.

THE JINUO

The Jinuo People are the most recent group in China to be recognized as a distinct minority nationality. Before this official status was granted them by the central government in Beijing, the Jinuo, though known as hill-dwellers who subsisted primarily by slash-and-burn agriculture, lived largely out of reach of state aid programs. Today their lot has improved considerably. They number around 12,000 and live in approximately 40 villages of the Jinuoluoke Mountains. Their homeland is also known as Youleshan.

The main settlement of Jinuoluoke lies 20 kilometres (12.5 miles) southeast of Mengyang on the road to the Tropical Botanical Garden at Xiaomenglun. The Jinuo celebrate their New Year Drum Dance Festival each January or early February, depending on the lunar calendar.

MENGYANG

Mengyang lies on the main road going north from Jinghong to Simao. There is a famous banyan here, a huge tree with roots shaped like an elephant; it is called the Elephant Tree. Nearby are villages of the Flower-Belt Dai and to the southeast lies the mountain home of the Jinuo.

TROPICAL BOTANICAL GARDEN AT XIAOMENGLUN

Thrusting deep into a bend of the Luosuo River is a narrow peninsula fancifully named Calabash Island (Huludao). There is nothing fanciful, however, about its 3,000 species of plants, one of the richest botanical concentrations in the world.

This is the home of Xishuangbanna's Tropical Botanical Garden, an institution founded in 1958 by dedicated scientists who simply set up shop in the jungle. Today there are nearly 500 workers who conduct important research in the areas of medicinal plants, taxonomy, economic plants and biochemistry.

For visitors who are not specialists, visiting here is like stepping into a bizarre and enchanted garden. A canopy of giant palms blocks out the sun, thick lily pads act as boats for children, camphor trees fill the air with pungency, large bamboos reach heavenward. There is edification as well as pleasure; many plant species at the Botanical Garden carry nameplates to explain their usefulness to man and nature.

Xiaomenglong lies 103 kilometres (65 miles) southeast of Jinghong.

MENGLA

The town and county seat of Mengla was the last region of Xishuangbanna to be opened to foreign travellers. It lies at the heart of a spur of land that thrusts into Laos, and has become popular as stepping off point for visiting Yao, Aini and Dai minority villages in the surrounding countryside; the sweet little settlement of Mamushi, northwest of Mengla, seems to hold the most promise.

Mengla itself is largely Sinicized, though the trip down from Jinghong—along the Mekong to Menghan, through jungle and rubber plantations to Mengxing, then south on the main road—is worth the trip for the fresh, wild scenery.

Man with traditional fishing equipment near the Stone Forest

THE EUNUCH ADMIRAL

In the year 1381, a ten-year-old Muslim boy named Ma Ho played among the fishing boats of his village, Kunyang, and dreamt that Lake Dianchi was a boundless ocean. His father and grandfather had made the pilgrimage to Mecca, at Asia's farthest limit, and had told rousing tales of the seas beyond China. The distinguished family, descended from an early Mongol governor of Yunnan, still remained loyal to the dynasty of Kublai Khan, and helped Yunnan put up resistance to the new Ming Dynasty that had seized power in China.

That year, a Ming army stormed into Yunnanfu, as Kunming was then called, and encircled Lake Dianchi, sweeping up captives. Ma Ho was seized, along with other boys, castrated, and sent into the army as an orderly. By the age of 20, the bright lad had become a junior officer, skilled at war and diplomacy. His abilities won him influential friends who helped him move to Nanjing, China's capital, during a turbulent period of wars and revolts. There he gained power and prestige as a court eunuch and the emperor gave him a new name—Cheng Ho or, as now spelled, Zheng He.

For 300 years, China had been extending its seaborne power, building up widespread commerce, importing spices, aromatics and raw materials from different parts of Asia. The arts of shipbuilding and navigation reached their height during the early Ming Dynasty. In 1405, the emperor appointed Zheng He as 'Commander-in-Chief of All Missions to the Western Seas', whereupon the eunuch admiral set sail on a mission of exploration and trade. He took 62 ships carrying 27,800 men—the largest naval fleet in the world at that time. It was the first of seven far-flung voyages that took him to the Indian Ocean, Persia, Arabia and the east coast of Africa.

On his fourth trip, Zheng He visited every major port of South and Southeast Asia and brought back envoys from more than 30 states to forge diplomatic relations and pay homage to the emperor of China. After the ambassadors had resided for six years in the new capital of Beijing, Zheng He made another voyage and took them all home again.

Thanks to Zheng He's genius, China held power over much of maritime Asia for half a century. However, China never established a trading empire, in contrast to the European nations who soon began exploring the earth's oceans, too. Instead, Zheng He's discoveries encouraged Chinese emigrants to settle in foreign countries, where their communities have flourished ever since.

Zheng He's atlases, logs and charts bequeathed a priceless record to the world and made maritime history. On his seventh and last voyage, between 1431 and 1433, Zheng He revisited all the distant places he had discovered 25 years earlier. He died in 1435, honoured throughout China but best beloved by the people of the southwest in the land of his birth, Yunnan.

A GUIDE TO PRONOUNCING CHINESE NAMES

The official system of romanization used in China, which the visitor will find on maps, road sign and city shopfronts, is known as Pinyin. It is now almost universally adopted by the western media.

Non-Chinese may initially encounter some difficulty in pronouncing romanized Chinese words. In fact many of the sounds correspond to the usual pronunciation of the letters in English. The exceptions are:

INITIALS

c	is like the ts in 'its'
q	is like the ch in 'cheese'
x	has no English equivalent, and can best be described as a hissing consonant that lies somewhere between sh and s. The sound was rendered as hs under an earlier transcription system.
z	is like the ds in 'fads'
zh	is unaspirated, and sounds like the j in 'jug'

FINALS

a	sounds like 'ah' as in 'father'
e	is pronounced as in 'her'
i	is pronounced as in 'ski'

(written as yi when not preceded by an initial consonant). However, in ci, chi, ri, shi, zi and zhi, the sound represented by the i final is quite different and is similar to the ir in 'sir', but without much stressing of the r syllable

o	sounds like the aw in 'law'
u	sounds like the oo in 'ooze'
ê	is pronounced as in 'get'
ü	is pronounced as the German ü (written as yu when not preceded by an initial consonant).

The last two finals are usually written simply as e and u.

FINALS IN COMBINATION

When two or more finals are combined, such as in hao, jiao and liu, each letter retains its sound value as indicated in the list above, but note the following:

ai	is like the ie in 'tie'
ei	is like the ay in 'bay'
ian	is like the ien in 'Vienna'
ie	similar to 'ear'
ou	is like the o in 'code'
uai	sounds like 'why'
uan	is like the uan in 'iguana'

(except when preceded by j, q, x and y; in these cases a u following any of these four consonants is in fact ü and uan is similar to uen.)

ue	is like the ue in 'duet'
ui	sounds like 'way'

EXAMPLES

A few Chinese names are shown below with English phonetic spelling beside them:

Beijing	Bay-jing	Cixi	Tsi-shi
Guilin	Gway-lin	Hangzhou	Hahng-jo
Kangxi	Kahn-shi	Qianlong	Chien-lawng
Tiantai	Tien-tie	Xi'an	Shi-ahn

An apostrophe is used to separate syllables in certain compound-character words to preclude confusion. For example, Changan (which can be chang-an or chan-gan) is sometimes written as Chang'an.

TONES

A Chinese syllable consists of not only an initial and a final or finals, but also a tone or pitch of the voice when the words are spoken. In Pinyin the four basic tones are marked ‾, ′, ˇ and ‵. These marks are almost never shown in printed form except in language texts.

A CHRONOLOGY OF PERIODS IN CHINESE HISTORY

Palaeolithic .... c.600,000–7000 BC
Neolithic .... c.7000–1600 BC
Shang .... c1600–1027 BC
Western Zhou... 1027–771 BC
Eastern Zhou .... 770–256 BC
Spring and Autumn Annals .... 770–476 BC
Warring States .... 475–221 BC
Qin .... 221–206 BC
Western (Former) Han 206BC–AD 8
Xin 9–24
Eastern (Later) Han 25–220
Three Kingdoms....................................... 220–265
Western Jin... 265–316
Northern and Southern Dynasties 317–589
Sixteen Kingdoms 317–439
Former Zhao 304–329
Former Qin 351–383
Later Qin 384–417
Northern Wei 386–534
Western Wei.. 535–556
Northern Zhou... 557–581
Sui 581–618
Tang... 618–907
Five Dynasties... 907–960
Northern Song... 960–1127
Southern Song... 1127–1279
Jin (Jurchen) 1115–1234
Yuan (Mongol) 1279–1368
Ming... 1368–1644
Qing (Manchu) 1644–1911
Republic of China 1911–1949
People's Republic of China....................... 1949–

Threshing ground at Dali

Practical Information

Hotels

Every effort has been made to list as much up-to-date information in this section as possible. Larger hotels requiring reservations are listed here with phone and, where possible, fax numbers. In the case of smaller hotels no phone or fax details have been listed since reservations are not normally required.

KUNMING 昆明

Begonia Hotel (*Haitang Fandian*)
Huancheng Dong Lu, 650000
Tel: (0871)3137573
海棠饭店 环城东路
231 rooms and suites. Located next to the Eastern Bus Station. General facilities, plus indoor swimming pool.

Golden Dragon Hotel
(*Jinlong Fandian*)
575 Beijing Lu, 650011
Tel: (0871)3133015
Fax: (0871)3131082
金龙饭店 北京路575号
Four star. 302 rooms and suites. Hong Kong-China joint venture. Restaurants offering Western, Japanese, Cantonese and local cuisine. Conference/banquet rooms, business centre, indoor swimming pool, gym, karaoke, disco, tennis court, clinic and a bar on the top floor with the best views of Kunming. Both CAAC and Dragonair have offices here.

Golden Flower Hotel
(*Jinhua Binguan*)
143 Huancheng Xi Lu, 650031
Tel: (0871)3132118

金花宾馆 环城西路143号
152 rooms and 17 suites. Chinese and Western restaurants, banquet hall, ballroom, bar.

Golden Peacock Hotel
(*Jinkongque Fandian*)
Daguan Lou 650032
Tel: (0871)4141298
Fax: (0871)4141087
金孔雀饭店 大观路
104 rooms. Lies outside of the city by Daguan Park. Restaurant, banquet hall, conference rooms, business centre, bar, billiard room, swimming pool, tennis courts, dance hall, karaoke.

Green Lake Hotel (*Cuihu Binguan*)
6 Cuihu Nan Lu, 650031
Tel: (0871)5155788
Fax: (0871)5153286
翠湖宾馆 翠湖南路6号
478 rooms and suites. New Wing completed in 1993. Pleasant location in city centre by Green Lake. Restaurants, banquet facilties, beauty salon, massage, tennis courts, business centre, clinic, excellent shopping arcade and restaurants.

Holiday Inn Kunming
(*Yinghua Jiari Jiudian*)
25 Dongfeng Dong Lu,
Tel: (0871)3165888   Fax: (0871)3131082
樱花假日大酒店 东风东路25号
Among Kunming's finest hotels this is
one of the newest in the Holiday Inn fleet.
Completed in 1993 it has 252 rooms,
seven restaurants, banqueting hall, swimming pool, health club and sauna.

King World Hotel (*Jinhua Da Jiudian*)
28 Beijing Nan Lu, 650011 Tel: (0871)
3138888 Fax: (0871)3138656, 3131910
锦华大酒店 北京路南段28号
Four Star. One of Kunming's newest
and best hotels. 320 rooms and suites.
Closest location of all hotels to the railway and bus stations. Chinese and
Western restaurants, revolving rooftop
restaurant, coffee shop, bar, business
centre, shopping arcade, banquet hall,
disco, function room, massage, beauty
salon, karaoke.

Kunhu Hotel (*Kunhu Fandian*)
Beijing Lu Tel: (0871)3133799
昆湖饭店 北京路
Only conveniently located budget hotel left in Kunming. Four-bed dorm
rooms with common shower and cheap
doubles with or without bath. Good location on Beijing Lu. Near to train and
bus stations, international post office
and next to backpackers' Happy Cafe.

Kunming Camellia Hotel
(*Kunming Chahua Binguan*)
154 Dongfeng Dong Lu, 650041
Tel: (0871)3163000, 3162918
昆明茶花宾馆 东风东路154号

140 rooms. Chinese restaurant, business centre, shopping arcade, dance
hall, bar. Reasonably priced, two-star
hotel. No longer a budget hotel.

Kunming Hotel (*Kunming Fandian*)
145 Dongfeng Dong Lu, 650051
Tel: (0871)3138220, 3162171
Fax; (0871)3163784
昆明饭店 东风东路145号
Four star. 400 rooms and suites. Chinese and Western restaurants, banquet
and conference rooms, coffee shop,
dance hall, gym, business centre,
karaoke, disco, sauna, beauty salon,
indoor swimming pool, shopping arcade, billiard room. Poste restante facilities. Bike hire.

Orchid Hotel (*Lanhua Binguan*)
Huancheng Nan Lu
Tel: (0871)3135553
Fax: (0871)3133155
兰花宾馆 环城南路
Opened 1992. 252 rooms. Restaurants,
karaoke, bar, dance hall, beauty salon.

Three Leaves Hotel (*Sanye Fandian*)
Beijing Lu Tel: (0871) 3512418
三叶饭店 北京路
No longer has dormitory accommodation, but has good location near train
and bus stations. Moderately priced.
Two star.

Yunnan Hotel (*Yunnan Fandian*)
83 Dongfeng Xi Lu.
Tel: (0871)3132419
云南饭店 东风西路83号
382 rooms. Restaurants, conference
room, shops, beauty salon, clinic.

STONE FOREST 石林
Stone Forest Hotel (*Shilin Binguan*)
Stone Forest
石林宾馆
This somewhat rustic hotel has 76 double rooms with private baths attached. Triples and singles are also available. The main building has a resthouse (*xiuxishi*) which contains a bar and performance hall for the nightly song and dance show of the local Sani minority. This is well worth attending. Numerous shops in and around the hotel and car park area sell Sani handicrafts, especially embroidered clothing, bags, shoes, and children's hats.

Yunlin Hotel (*Yunlin Fandian*)
Stone Forest
云林饭店
Near the Shilin Binguan, has a fair share of budget accommodation. These two hotels are frequently full between the months of August and October. A bed can always be found in the hostels surrounding the bus station near the car park. These hostels are spartan and cheap.

DALI REGION 大理
Dali Hotel (*Dali Binguan*)
Fuxing Lu, Dali Tel: (0872)2670386
Fax: (0872)2670551
大理宾馆
Budget to moderate accommodation. Back building has pleasant old wooden rooms for the economically minded.

Erhai Guesthouse (*Erhai Binguan*)
140 Renmin Lu , Xiaguan
Tel: (0872)2125896
洱海宾馆 下关人民路140号

This is the main hotel for foreign tourists in Xiaguan.

Keyun Hotel (*Keyun Fandian*)
Next to the bus station in Xiaguan.
Tel: (0872)2122173
客运饭店 建设路
Budget to moderate accommodation.

Nanzhao Hotel (*Nanzhao Binguan*)
Jianshe Lu, Dali Tel: (0872)2121913
南诏宾馆

Number Two Guesthouse
(*Di Er Zhaodaisuo*)
Huguo Lu, Dali Tel: (0872)2670309
第二招待所 护国路
Budget to moderate accommodation, the cheapest rooms in lovely old but noisy wooden buildings are in the original section of the guesthouse. A popular hotel among budget travellers. Bicycle rental in courtyard. Small booth just inside the gate sells bus tickets and excursions to surrounding areas.

Sunny Garden Hotel
Huguo Lu, Dali
大理护国路
Just up the street from Number 2 Guesthouse. Good, clean and cheap three to four bed rooms. Shared showers. Pleasant atmosphere

Xiaguan Hotel (*Xiaguan Binguan*)
Jianshe Lu, Xiaguan 671000
Tel: (0872)2124531
下关宾馆 建设路
154 rooms. Opened 1988. Located in the city centre. Meeting rooms, Chinese and Western restaurants. Shopping arcade.

Xizhou Villa (*Xizhou Tianzhuang*)
Xizhou, on Erhai Lake.
Tel Dali switchboard.
喜洲天庄

LIJIANG 丽江
Lijiang Guesthouse (*Lijiang Binguan*)
Also known as No.1 Guesthouse
(*Di Yi Zhaodaisuo*)
Xin Da Jie
丽江宾馆 新大街
New and Old Wings, budget to moderate rates. Bike rental. Travel services. Located across the street from the regional government offices, off Xin Dajie.

Number Two Guesthouse
(*Di Er Zhaodaisuo*)
丽江第二招待所
Situated inside gate behind old North Bus Station and opposite the Main Square. New and Old Wings, budget to moderate rates. Good location.

Yunshan Hotel (*Yunshan Fandian*)
Also known as No. 3 Guesthouse (*Di San Zhaodaisuo*) Tel: (0888)5121315
云杉饭店
Next to main bus station. This is a good hotel though inconveniently located far away from the center of town. Since bus companies now pick up customers at their ticket offices in the center of town it is no longer needed to live near the bus station.

Grand Lijiang Hotel,
Xinyi Street, Dayan Town 674100 Lijiang
Tel: (0888)5121102
丽江大饭店
Best standard hotel. With 50 rooms plus two restaurants.

DAJU 大具
Tiger Leaping Gorge Hotel
(*Hutiaoxia Lushe*)
虎跳峡旅社

QIAOTOU 桥头
Qiaotou Guesthouse (*Qiaotou Binguan*)
桥头宾馆

ZHONGDIAN 中甸
Yongsheng Hotel (*Yongsheng Fandian*)
永胜饭店

Kangben Minorities Hotel
(*Kangben Minzu Jiulou*)
Tel: (0887)8222091
康奔民族酒楼
Commonly known as the Minzu Hotel.

Transport Hostel
(*Jiaotong Zhaodaisuo*)
Tel: (0887)8806096
交通招待所

Zhongdian Hostel
(*Zhongdian Zhaodaisuo*)
Tel: (0887)8222932
中甸招待所

CHUXIONG 楚雄
Chuxiong Hotel
9 Xinshijie Tel: (0878)3123592
楚雄宾馆 新大街9号

Zixi Hotel
(Guesthouse of the Chuxiong Municipal Government) 200 Fuhuo Jie
Tel: (0878)3123613
紫溪宾馆 府后街200号
Both hotels have restaurants that serve local dishes.

JIANGCHUAN 江川
Jiangchuan County Guesthouse
(*Jiangchuan Xian Binguan*)
Tel: (0877)8013223
江川宾馆

GEJIU 个旧
Jinhu Hotel (*Jinhu Binguan*)
Building No. 10 Hotel
Tel: (0873)2123348
金湖宾馆

JIANSHUI 建水
Guihu Guesthouse (*Guihu Binguan*)

QUJING 曲靖
Unicorn Guesthouse (*Qilin Binguan*)
Nanning Lu Tel: (0874)3122390
麒麟宾馆

Qujing Guesthouse (*Qujing Binguan*)
Wenchang Lu
曲靖宾馆

TONGHAI 通海
Xiushan Hotel (*Xiushan Fandian*)

SHAPING 沙坪
Shaping Guesthouse
(*Shaping Xian Zhaodaisuo*)
沙坪宾馆

XISHUANGBANNA 西双版纳
JINGHONG 景洪
Banna Hotel (*Banna Binguan*)
Sometimes known as the **No. 1 Guest-
house (*Di Yi Zhaodaisuo*)**
11 Galan Zhong Lu
Tel: (0691)2126429
第一招待所 版纳宾馆 嘎兰路11号
Two star. 100 rooms. Restaurant serv-

ing local cuisine. Main hotel for tourists in Jinghong. Attractively priced
three-bed rooms with shower and
cheap dorm beds in the Bamboo
House section.

There are several Dai guesthouses on
Manting Lu. The **Wanli Dai Restaurant**
has dorm beds and simple facilities at
very cheap prices. The **Lotus Hotel** on
the same street offers similar accommodations.

Communications Hotel
(*Jiaotong Fandian*)
交通饭店
Next to the long-distance bus station. It
is overlooked by most, but offers pleasant, moderately priced accommodation.

Banna Mansion (*Banna Dasha*)
版纳大厦
Offers up-market accommodation in
the heart of town.

Bamboo Cottages Guesthouse
(*Zhulou Binguan*)
Tropical Crops Research Institute. 28
Jinghong Xi Lu Tel: (0691)2127802
竹楼宾馆

Yilan Yilan Holiday Village
(*Yilan Yilan Du Jia Chuan*)
Tel: (0691)2126050
依兰依兰渡假村
Outside entrance to Tropical Crops Research Institute. Mid-range accommodation in Dai style bungalow.

MENGHAN (GANLANBA) 勐罕
Dai Bamboo House in the centre of

town offers spartan accommodation in a traditional Dai family setting.
傣家竹楼

Ganlanba State Agricultural Guest-house (*Ganlanba Guoyi Nongchang Zhaodaisuo***)**
橄榄坝 国营农场招待所

DAMENGLONG 大孟力龙
Damenglong Guesthouse (*Damenglong Zhaodaisuo***)**
大孟力龙招待所
Extremely spartan accommodation.

MENGHAI 孟力海
Menghai County Guesthouse (*Menghai Xian Binguan***)**
Tel: (0691)5122429
孟力海县宾馆
Simple accommodation in classic Chinese government guesthouse.

MENGHUN 孟力混
White Tower Hotel and **Phoenix Hotel (***Fenghuang Fandian***)** by market area.
白塔饭店和凤凰饭店

SIMAO 思茅
Simao Hotel (*Simao Binguan***)**
Zhengxing Lu Tel: (0879)2124804
思茅宾馆

MENGLUN 孟力仑
Menglun Botanical Garden Hostel (*Menglun Zhiwuyuan Zhaodaisuo***)**
Xiao Menglun, Tropical Plants Institute
孟力仑植物园招待所

DEHONG AREA AND WESTERN YUNNAN
BAOSHAN 保山

Baoshan Guesthouse (*Baoshan Binguan***)**
Shangxiang Jie
Tel: (0875)2122804, 2122393
保山宾馆 上巷街
20 minute walk from bus station. Pleasant old-style government hotel.

Yindou Hotel (*Yindou Da Jiudian***)**
Baoxiu Dong Lu
Tel: (0875)2120939, 2120948
保山银都大酒店 保岫东路
Probably the smartest hotel in town, with accordingly high prices.

LUXI (MANSHI) 潞西
Dehong Guesthouse (*Dehong Binguan***)**
Tel: (0692)2122169
德宏宾馆 友谊路58号
Dorm and standard rooms.

RUILI 瑞丽
Ruili Guesthouse (*Ruili Binguan***)**
Tel: (0692)4141463
瑞丽宾馆 新建路15号
Old rambling style hotel with guesthouse feeling. Has dorm and standard accommodation. Located off Xingshi Lu market area.

Mingrui Hotel (*Mingrui Binguan***)**
31 Nanmao Jie Tel: (0692)4148795
明瑞宾馆 南卯街31号
Good value hotel. Clean and cheap with convenient location near bus station. Three-bed rooms and nice doubles.

Yongchang Hotel (*Yongchang Da Jiudian***)**
Renmin Lu Tel: (0692)4141804
永昌大酒店 人民路
Dorm and regular rooms. Also good value.

Nanyang Hotel (*Nanyang Binguan*)
Nanmao Jie
Tel: (0692)4141766
南洋宾馆　南卯街
Good location on main street; stiff prices.

WANDING 畹町
**Wanding Guesthouse
(*Wanding Binguan*)**
Tel: (0692)5151327
畹町宾馆
Pleasant hotel with good views of Burma, but somewhat inconvenient location.

Yufeng Hotel (*Yufeng Dalou*)
Cheap, clean, friendly and in the center of this small town.

TENGCHONG 腾冲
**Tengchong Guesthouse
(*Tengchong Binguan*)**
12 Guanting Xiang
Tel: (0875)5121044
腾冲宾馆　官厅巷12号

No. 4 Government Hotel (*Di Si Lushe*)
Yingjiang Dong Lu
第四旅社

Useful Addresses

AIRLINE OFFICES
Civil Aviation Administration Of China (CAAC)
146 Dongfeng Dong Lu
Reservations tel: (0871)3164270
Cargo tel: (0871)3137888
中国民航　东风东路146号

China Yunnan Airlines
146 Dongfeng Dong Lu
Tel: (0871)3164415
Fax: (0871)3168437
中国云南航空公司　东风东路146号

Dragonair
Golden Dragon Hotel, 575 Beijing Lu
Tel: (0871)3149208
港龙航空公司　北京路575号

BANKS
Bank of China (Kunming Branch)
270–271 Huguo Lu
Tel: (0871)3179345 Telex. 64034
中国银行昆明分行　护国路270–271号

**People's Bank of China
(Yunnan Branch)**
180 Zhengyi Lu Tel: (0871)3164143
中国人民银行云南分行　正义路180号

CINEMAS AND THEATRES
Hongxing Theatre
Dongfeng Xi Lu Tel: (0871)3165275
红星剧院　东风西路180号

Kunming Theatre
Qingnian Lu Tel: (0871)3165583
昆明剧院　青年路180号

Panlong Theatre
202 Baoshan Jie Tel: (0871)3162639
盘龙电影场　宝善街202号

Xinghuo Theatre
Baoshan Jie Tel: (0871)3133181
星火剧院　宝善街

HOSPITALS
Kunming Number One Affliated Hospital
Huancheng Xi Lu Tel: (0871)5324888
昆明医学院第一附属医院 环城西路

Yunnan Number One People's Hospital
173 Jinbi Lu Tel: (0871)3161030
云南第一人民医院 金碧路173号

MUSEUMS
Yunnan Provincial Museum
2 Wuyi Lu Tel: (0871)3163694
云南省博物馆 五一路2号

POST AND TELECOMMUNICATIONS
Post Office (Youzheng Ju)
555 Beijing Lu Tel: (0871)3133749
昆明邮局 北京路555号

Main Post Office (Youdian Ju)
Dongfeng Dong Lu at Beijing Lu
Tel: (0871)3168013
昆明邮电局 东风东路

PUBLIC SECURITY BUREAU
Public Affairs Bureau (Gonganju)
Foreign Affairs Section
525 Beijing Lu Tel: (0871)3161021
昆明市公安外事科 北京路525号
(open 8–12 am, 2–6 pm)

SHOPS
ANTIQUE, ARTS AND CRAFTS
Friendship Store
99 Dongfeng Xi Lu
Tel: (0871)3613531
友谊商店 东风西路99号

Yunnan Arts and Crafts Shop
Tel: (0871)3166871
云南省工艺美术服务部

Yunnan Antiques and Curios
Keji Dalou, Nantaiqiao
Tel: (0871)3161296
云南文物商店 南太桥科技大楼

DEPARTMENT STORES
**Kunming Department Store
(Kunming Baihuo Da Lou)**
Dongfeng Xi Lu Tel:(0871)3136449
昆明百货大楼 东风西路

**Dongfeng Department Store
(Dongfeng Baihuo Shangdian)**
Dongfeng Xi Lu Tel: (0871)3133319
东风百货商店 东风西路

**Minorities Department Store
(Minzu Maoyi Dalou)**
Dongfeng Lu Tel: (0871)3165935
(Special shop for tourists upstairs)
昆明民族贸易大楼 东风路

BOOKS
Foreign Languages Bookstore
Keji Dalou, Nantaiqiao
Tel: (0871)3312983
外文书店 南太桥科技大楼

Kunming Xinhua Bookstore
Nanping Jie Tel: (0871)3164492
昆明市新华书店 南屏街

Yunnan Xinhua Bookstore
Wujingqiao Tel: (0871)3133028
云南省新华书店 吴井桥

MISCELLANEOUS
Zhengyi Photographic Shop
109 Zhengyi Lu
Tel: (0871)3132111
正义照相器材商店 昆明市正义路109号

TRAVEL AND TRANSPORT

KUNMING

China Travel Service (Yunnan)
6/F, Zhong Ming Plaza
36 Beijing Road
Kunming
Tel: (0871)3174366 Fax: 3179878

Diethelm Travel
Diethelm are planning to open offices
in Kunming, Dali, Lijiang and Jinghong.
Please see Thailand entry on page 197.

**Yunnan Exploration & Amusement
   Travel Co Ltd**
1/F, North Section of Building B
73 Renmin West Road
Kunming
Tel: (0871)5312283 Fax: 5312324

Kunming Airport
Wujiaba
Tel: (0871)3132675
(7.5 kilometres/4.6 miles from town)
昆明机场 巫家坝

China Travel Service
6th Floor, Zhong Ming Plaza Kunming
Tel: 3515268 Fax: 3179878/4086
中国旅行社昆明分社

Kunming Railway Station
Nanyao (southern end of Beijing Lu)
Enquiries tel: (0871)3511534
Baggage tel: (0871)3165469
昆明火车站 南窑

Kunming Taxi Co.
45 Beijing Lu Tel: (0871)3137607
昆明市出租汽车公司 北京路45号

DALI

Overseas Travel Corp. (OTC)
141 Renmin Lu, Xiaguan 671000.
海外旅行社 下关人民路141号

RUILI

Overseas Travel Corp. (OTC)
Rm 203 Mingrui Hotel
31 Nanmao Lu 678600
Tel: (0692)4148795 ext.203
Fax: (0692)4143223
瑞丽海外旅行社

XISHUANGBANNA

China Yunnan Airlines
Civil Aviation Building, Jungde Road,
Jinghong
Tel: (08838)24774,' (00662) 2797070
中国云南航空公司

CITS
12 Galan Zhong Lu, Jinghong 650011
Tel: (0691)2122152 Fax:(0691)2125980
Offer numerous tours in area. Good
local information and helpful staff.
西双版纳中国国际旅行社

SPECIALIST TRAVEL OPERATORS

Not all these companies may offer Yunnan in their itineraries but they are specialists in exotic destinations.

THAILAND
Diethelm Travel
Kian Gwan Building, 140/1 Wireless Road, Bangkok 10330
Tel: (662)255–9150/60
Fax: (662)256–0248/49

SINGAPORE
China Yunnan Airlines
137 Cecil Street, ICS Building #01–02, Singapore 069537
Tel: 3240188 Fax: 3240166
中国云南航空公司

PEOPLE'S REPUBLIC OF CHINA
China Travel Service (HK) Ltd
Foreign Passenger Department
4/F, CTS House, 78–83 Connaught Rd, Central, Hong Kong
Tel: (852)28533888 Fax: 25419777
香港中国旅行社 干诺道中78–83号

Abercrombie & Kent
19F, Gitic Centre, 28 Queens Road East, Wanchai, Hong Kong
Tel: (852)28657818
Fax: (852)28660556

UNITED KINGDOM
Regent Holidays UK Ltd
15 John Street
Bristol BS1 2HR
Tel: (01179)211711,
Fax: (01179)254866

ACE Study Tours
Babraham
Cambridge CB2 4AP
Tel: (01233)835055
Fax: (01233)837394

Occidor Adventure Tours Limited
10 Broomcroft Road
Bognor Regis, West Sussex PO22 7NJ
Tel: (01243)582178
Fax: (01243)587239

Travelsphere Ltd
Compass House
Rockingham Road
Market Harborough
Leicestershire LE16 7QD
Tel: (01858)410818
Fax: (01243)587239

UNITED STATES
Abercrombie & Kent International
Oak Brook, Illinois
Tel: (630)9542944, (800)3237308

American Museum of Natural History Discovery Tours
New York, N.Y.
Tel: (212)7695700, (800)4628687
www.amnh.org

Asian Pacific Adventures
Los Angeles, California
Tel: (213)9353156, (800)8251680

Bryan World Tours
Topeka, Kansas
Tel: (913)2727511, (800)2553507

Geographic Expeditions
San Francisco, California
Tel: (415)9220448, (800)7778183

Mountain Travel-Sobek
El Cerrito, California
Tel: (510)5278100, (800)2272384
www.mtsobek.com

Smithsonian Study Tours
Washington, D.C.
Tel: (202)3574700
www.si.edu/tsa/sst

TCS Expeditions
Seattle, Washington
Tel: (206)7277300, (800)7277477

Travcoa
Newport Beach, California
Tel: (714)4762800, (800)9922003

Wilderness Travel
Berkeley, California
Tel: (510)5480420, (800)3682794

AUSTRALIA
Adventure World
101 Great South Road
73 Walker Street, North Sydney
NSW 2060
Tel: (2)9567766, toll free 008 221 931
Fax: (2)9567707

(Melbourne Branch)
3rd Floor, 343 Little Collins Street
Melbourne, VIC 3000
Tel: (2)6700125, toll free 008 133322
Fax: (2)6707707

Index of Places in Yunnan